Red Hugh

The extraordinary story of Hugh O'Donnell,
son of The O'Donnell, chieftain of Donegal,
who was captured and
held prisoner in Dublin Castle

a real-life adventure

'well written, with pace and excitement.
It is no surprise that this book won an award.'
The Irish Times

'A true story and a ripping yarn.'
RTE Guide

'Warring chieftains, castle dungeons, camaraderie
and stoic endurance are all elements in this story of
adventure and derring-do.'
Best Books

**For Vincent, Annette and Rory,
and most of all for Colm
who kissed a lady and made her
feel very special**

RED HUGH

Deborah Lisson

THE O'BRIEN PRESS
DUBLIN

This edition first published in Ireland 1999
by The O'Brien Press Ltd.
20 Victoria Road, Dublin 6, Ireland.
Tel. +353 1 4923333; Fax. +353 1 4922777
email: books@obrien.ie; website: www.obrien.ie
Reprinted 2000

ISBN: 0-86278-604-5

Originally published in 1998 by Thomas C. Lothian Pty Ltd.
11 Munro Street, Port Melbourne, Victoria 3207, Australia

British Library Cataloguing-in-Publication Data
Lisson, Deborah
Red Hugh
1.O'Donnell, Hugh Roe - Juvenile fiction 2.Bibliographical fiction
3.Children's stories
823.9'14[J]

2 3 4 5 6 7 8 9 10
00 01 02 03 04 05 06 07

The O'Brien Press receives
assistance from

The Arts Council
An Chomhairle Ealaíon

Layout and design: The O'Brien Press Ltd.
Colour separations: C&A Print Services Ltd.
Printing: Cox & Wyman Ltd.

contents

Ireland in the XVI Century

background

THIS BOOK OPENS in the year 1587, during the latter part of the reign of Queen Elizabeth I. It was a time when England was tightening her control over Ireland and making a concerted effort to break, once and for all, the power of the Gaelic chieftains. To a great extent this had already been accomplished in the three southern provinces of Munster, Leinster and Connaught. However, Ulster, the northern province, was proving more troublesome.

Remote and inaccessible, it was still largely 'untamed'. Real power rested in the hands of two families – O'Donnell in Tír Chonaill (modern-day Donegal) and O'Neill in Tír Eoin (Tyrone). They were traditional enemies and this had always worked to the advantage of the English administration. But by 1587 this situation appeared to be changing.

Hugh mac Manus, the incumbent O'Donnell, was failing mentally and physically, and his people – the Cenél Chonaill – were split in their support of a successor. Under Irish law, succession did not automatically pass to the eldest son as it did in England. Instead it went to an already elected heir (the *tánaiste*) the 'oldest and ablest' man within a defined kinship of the late chieftain. That was in theory, of course; in practice it more often went to the man who could raise the biggest army on the day and in 1587 that man looked increasingly likely to be O'Donnell's fifteen-year-old son, Hugh Roe – the Red Hugh of this story.

In Tyrone, the incumbent O'Neill, Turlough Luineach, was a drunkard, in poor health and not expected to live much longer. Rivalry was intense between his potential successors too. In a bid for support, the ablest of them, Hugh mac Ferdoragh O'Neill, Second Earl of Tyrone, had married O'Donnell's daughter Siobhán and was planning to betroth a daughter by his first marriage to the young Hugh Roe.

Faced with the prospect of a united and possibly unfriendly Ulster, Sir John Perrot, the English Lord Deputy in Dublin, decided that measures needed to be taken to ensure O'Donnell's continued loyalty to the crown. His first move was to demand hostages of O'Donnell as a pledge of his good faith.

Hostage-taking did not then carry the same sinister overtones it does today. It was an accepted and widely practised custom among the Irish themselves – newly inaugurated chieftains took 'pledges' from their sub-chieftains or unsuccessful rivals, and hostages would also be exchanged between rival chieftains before important meetings.

In theory, at least, these pledges were given freely and were often volunteers. Irish law also spelt out strict conditions for their treatment. They lived as honoured guests in the households of their hosts and – provided those for whom they stood pledge behaved themselves – were not regarded as prisoners.

The English, though, played by different rules. They demanded pledges but never gave any in return, and were not too fussy about how they treated their hostages. The account by Sir William Fitzwilliam (Perrot's successor as Lord Deputy) concerning the conditions under which even young children were held in Dublin Castle makes chilling reading. Hugh mac Ferdoragh O'Neill protested to the Council on one occasion that it would be impossible for him to find suitable volunteers if they were all to be locked up and treated as prisoners.

In 1586 Perrot extracted a promise from O'Donnell that he would send Hugh Roe's younger brother, Rory, to Dublin as a pledge. However, in the words I have put into the mouth of his wife, the Iníon Dubh: 'There is a wealth of difference between promise and intent.' When no hostage was forthcoming by the autumn of the following year, Perrot decided to take matters into his own hands. A ship, the *Matthew*, well stocked with wine and purporting to be on a voyage from Spain, was dispatched to Tír Chonaill on a secret mission. The consequences of that mission form the basis of this book.

One important aspect of sixteenth-century Anglo-Irish conflict is the religious question. Elizabeth was ruthless in attempting to stamp out Catholicism in Ireland and establish the Church of England in its place. Her reasons were political rather than theological. In part it was a cultural device – a means of anglicising and thereby 'civilising' a people she considered barbaric, but there was also a more pressing reason. England was at that time under real threat of invasion from Spain. Spain was a Catholic country and a natural ally of Ireland. Not only did they share the same faith, but the Irish believed themselves to be descended from Spanish ancestors – the Milesians of mythological history. Elizabeth feared that if her rebellious Irish subjects appealed for aid to Philip of Spain, he might use their country as a stepping stone for an invasion of England. Catholicism, therefore, was seen as synonymous with treason.

This, of course, is a very simplified outline of conditions. Sixteenth-century Irish history is a minefield of intrigue and confusion – volumes could be written on the conniving and double-dealing that occurred on both sides. It will, however give you some idea of the turbulent background against which the young Hugh Roe O'Donnell set out for Rathmullen on that fateful day in October 1587.

NOTE

At the end of the book you will find a Postscript about Red Hugh's life after the events of this story (page 212); a list of the main characters (page 214); the O'Neill and O'Donnell family trees (page 216-7); and a pronunciation guide to the Irish words (page 218).

one

HE IS DROWNING in Lough Swilly. The dark bubbling waters close above his head and thick weeds tangle his feet and draw him downward. He sinks unresisting – how peaceful it is to die. But he is cheating —it is not supposed to end like this. He has obligations. What are they? —he tries to remember them, but they float somewhere in the back of his mind and he cannot hold on to them.

Figures move round him in the water – pale, naked figures. Voices whisper to him.

'We died for you, Red Hugh, son of O'Donnell. Will you leave us unavenged?'

'When Hugh succeeds Hugh . . . the last Hugh shall be Árd Rí of all Ireland and drive all the foreigners out.'

'You were not born to die in an English prison.'

What do they want of him? They cling like cobwebs and he tries to shake them off. Ghostlike, they fade. But then there comes another voice – one he has never heard before. 'Where are the champions of Ulster?' it demands, echoing a question he once asked himself. 'Where are the champions of Ulster? Has the hero-light died in the heart of Ireland?'

'An English merchantman,' announced Donal Gorm MacSweeney, 'come into Lough Swilly out of Spain with a cargo of the best wine you ever tasted.' He glanced around the banqueting hall of Donegal Castle as though testing the effect of his words. 'And they practically giving it away to all-comers,' he finished dramatically.

His audience gazed at him in astonishment. 'In Lough Swilly?' repeated Hugh Dubh O'Donnell, 'and she an English vessel? What in the name of God brought her there?' He sounded a mite put out – jealous, perhaps, that the English merchant had chosen to honour The MacSweeney rather than himself.

'She is bound for Greenwich,' said Donal Gorm, 'but her skipper says isn't every ship coming into England these days carrying wines? He is looking for a more profitable cargo – and he after hearing that The O'Donnell is the best lord of fish in Ireland and willing to trade the same for good Spanish sack.'

'If he wanted to trade with me, why did he not come to Donegal or Killybegs?'

The young man's blue eyes twinkled. 'Sure didn't he think Rathmullen one of your castles, O'Donnell? But my father offers you the welcome of his hall and you coming to visit him. He promises you grand entertainment and all the wine you can carry away with you.'

'A generous offer,' said The O'Donnell. 'My sorrow that I must disappoint him. But I leave tomorrow for a meeting with the English Lord Deputy.'

'Oh.' Donal looked disappointed.

Two boys seated further down the table, who had been listening intently to the conversation, began to whisper to one another. The younger one dug his companion in the ribs. 'Go on, Eoghan, I dare you.'

The older boy stood up. 'Why don't I go in your place, O'Donnell?' he suggested boldly. 'Sure and won't O'Neill be sending his own men for the wine and we not buying it first? And small joy it would be, I'm thinking, to see it going down that throat like slops into a cesspit.'

Everyone laughed – they knew the drinking habits of Turlough Luineach O'Neill. Even The O'Donnell had to smile. He looked enquiringly at the tall, silver-haired man sitting at his right hand. 'Well, O'Gallagher, is this young cub of yours to be trusted with such a mission?'

Eoghan mac Toole O'Gallagher looked sternly at his son, then at his chieftain. He chuckled. 'Ah let him go, O'Donnell. He has a good head on his shoulders, for all his wildness – and forbye, won't it keep him out of mischief for a week or two.'

There was more laughter. Eoghan glanced at his companion. 'And Hugh Roe to go with me?' he asked hopefully.

The O'Donnell shook his head. 'Not Hugh,' he said. 'His place is here and I out of the country.'

'But, Father . . .' the younger boy turned beseeching eyes on the chieftain.

His father looked at him sternly. 'Your place is here, son. One day, God willing, you will succeed me. You must show the clans you are worthy to fill my place.'

The boy bit his lip. I have no wish for your place, he wanted to protest, and I with no right to it, anyway. I may be your son, but I am not your elected successor – your tánaiste. Your uncle, Hugh mac Hugh Dubh holds that office. But he kept his mouth shut. O'Donnell was his chieftain as well as his father, and a chieftain's decisions were not to be challenged. He turned his head, trying to hide his disappointment. Then, to his surprise, help came – from a most unexpected quarter.

'Let the lad go, Hugh,' coaxed the Lady Finnoula O'Donnell, laying a hand on her husband's arm. 'He is not after putting his foot on the inauguration stone yet. What harm to allow him a little freedom?'

Her husband looked at her in bewilderment. 'And you after insisting I bring him early out of fosterage – that I show the clans he carries my name in my absence.'

'Then let them see it. Let him ride in your name to Rathmullen and conduct your trade with this English merchant.'

The O'Donnell still looked doubtful, but Hugh knew the argument had been won. He flashed his mother a grateful grin and she smiled at him fondly. What an extraordinary woman she is, he thought. So fierce, so proud, so ruthless in her ambition, you would swear she had not a gentle bone in her body. Yet she loved him, and felt no shame to show it.

She loved her husband too, and that was even stranger, for Hugh mac Manus O'Donnell must surely try her patience at times. The chieftain was no longer the vigorous man she had married. He was aging, growing forgetful and indecisive – and people knew it. They whispered. Wasn't it really the Lady Finnoula – the Iníon Dubh, as they called her – who held the reins these days? And many of them resented that. Despite his reluctance to have himself intruded into a dynastic struggle, Hugh could understand the urgency to have it resolved.

He waited patiently for his father's pronouncement and, at last, The O'Donnell made up his mind. 'Very well,' he conceded, 'you may go with Eoghan and Donal. But no unseemly carousing, mind. You are to conduct yourself in a manner befitting a chieftain's son.'

'Oh, I will, Father.' Hugh grinned exultantly and punched Eoghan on the arm. His heart sang like a bird. A journey to Rathmullen – and with his two best friends for company. This adventure was going to be grand – almost as good as the day they had let him ride on his first cattle raid.

❀　❀　❀

They rode into Rathmullen Castle late the following afternoon. Donal MacSweeney Fanad came out to his gates with his wife to receive them. 'It's welcome you are at my hearth,' he greeted them, as his horseboys stepped forward to take the travellers' mounts. 'And look at yourself, Hugh Roe – out of fosterage, and dreaming, no doubt, of all the sins you're going to commit, now you are after escaping the clutches of The MacSweeney Doe.'

Hugh smiled. He had no quarrel with the Irish

custom of fosterage. He had enjoyed his years in the household of Eoghan MacSweeney Doe and the bonds he had forged with his foster family would stand him in good stead in the years to come. Nevertheless, the end of fosterage meant the end of childhood at last, and he had looked forward to the day when he would finally be reckoned a man. Answerable to no one and able to make his own decisions – that was what he had always assumed. But now it seemed . . . He pulled a face. 'Chance would be a fine thing,' he said, only half joking. 'Sure, isn't everyone still telling me what to do?'

His host laughed. 'A sad truth, lad. It's the circle of life. We eat ducks, ducks eat frogs, frogs eat worms and worms eat us – eventually. There is no man, however grand, does not have something nipping at his heels.'

'And what of Himself, then,' asked Eoghan cheekily. 'Who nips at the O'Donnell's heels?'

They looked at one another and laughed simultaneously. 'Herself it is,' chuckled MacSweeney. 'And, sure, isn't that the truth for every man and he married?'

'And you loving it,' chided his wife, elbowing him in the ribs. 'Boast and swagger all you will, would you not be missing me sorely now, and I not here to keep your affairs in order?'

'My sorrow, but I would,' confessed MacSweeney with feigned meekness. He winked at the boys. 'Never argue with a woman, lads. They have the tongues on them would shrivel a fire-breathing dragon in full blast.'

'Ha, and I meek as a harvest mouse.' The Lady

MacSweeney laughed heartily. 'But come away in, lads. It's tired you must be after your long ride. Shame on you, Donal, and you keeping them standing so long at your gates. Supper is preparing in the hall, and Donal Gorm shall show you to your quarters. They are sharing your chamber, Donal. I thought that would be best.'

Donal Gorm led them upstairs to his bedchamber. It was a large room at the top of the keep, overlooking Inch Island and the waters of Lough Swilly. Inside all had been made ready for them. Torches blazed in sconces on the wall, fresh rushes were spread on the floor and against one wall stood a huge feather bed piled with rugs and furs. The Lady MacSweeney knew how to look after her guests.

Eoghan kicked off his shoes and flung himself down on the bed. 'Ah, now, this is comfort,' he said. 'We'll sleep like kings tonight.' He grinned. 'And Hugh Roe, here, to sleep in the middle – he being the youngest – and we to poke him in the ribs and him snoring.'

'Ha!' Hugh snatched up a pillow and buffeted his friend across the face. 'Won't I remember that, O'Gallagher, should I ever come to the chieftaincy? A grand little dungeon I'll have, in my castle on Lough Eske, for those who insult The O'Donnell.'

He fell on Eoghan and dragged him to the floor and they wrestled till they were both too weak from laughter to continue. As they scrambled to their feet, Eoghan held up his hands in mock surrender. 'Ah, you have me beaten,' he pleaded and collapsed on the bed again. 'I'm killed entirely, just leave me here to rest in peace – but don't forget to call me at supper time.' And he folded his arms across his chest, shut his eyes and began to snore loudly.

Hugh and Donal laughed. Hugh crossed to the window and looked out at the lough, where the English ship rode at anchor, black and bulky against a darkening sky. There was something almost sepulchral in her beauty and her masts and rigging looked like the skeletons of winter trees. He shivered, without knowing why.

'She's called the *Matthew*,' said Donal Gorm, coming to stand beside him. 'And she after coming all the way from Spain. Would it not be grand to sail on her – to follow the winds around the world to harbour in Cadiz?'

Hugh nodded. He put his elbows on the windowsill and with his chin cupped in his hands leaned forward to have a better look. The *Matthew* rocked gently in the current, straining against her anchor as though eager to break free and follow the tide back to the open sea. He could see men moving about on her decks.

He tried to imagine Spain: a land of legend and mystery; of blue skies and eternal sunshine, where grape vines grew in orchards, like apple trees. The land of his ancestors. Thousands of years ago, Milesius and his followers had crossed the sea from Spain to settle in Ireland. He wondered what they had looked like, those ancient adventurers. The Spanish merchants he had met in his father's hall had all been dark – slim, elegant men, black-haired and dark-eyed. His father was dark too – maybe

Milesius had looked like him. But Hugh had never seen a Spaniard with red hair. Perhaps I get that from my mother's side, he thought.

'Were I High King of Ireland,' he said dreamily, 'wouldn't I build myself a ship like yon and sail to Spain in her? She'd have masts of gold and sails white as the wings of swans and I'd marry the King of Spain's daughter and carry her over the seas to Tír na nÓg.'

'Then, by God, you'd do it on your lone,' said Eoghan's voice from behind them. He sat up as they turned to look at him and swung his long legs over the side of the bed. 'If you've a mind to sail off to the otherworld with the King of Spain's daughter then leave me out of your plans. Sure, all I want out of Spain is a flagon of their good wine, and it sitting on the table before me in an honest Irish hall. I have a hunger and thirst on me like the Dagda at the Fomorian feast. Do they never remember you have a mouth in this place?'

'Ah, they do then,' said Donal, spluttering with laughter, 'though it's little enough you deserve, O'Gallagher, and you with no more poetry in you than a bull's backside.' And still chuckling he led them downstairs to the hall.

Supper was a lavish and leisurely meal, ample enough to satisfy even Eoghan's hunger. The MacSweeney Fanad was justly famed for his hospitality. He sat Hugh on his right hand and questioned him with interest about affairs in Donegal.

'So, your father is away to his meeting with Lord

Deputy Perrot,' he said. 'And The O'Neill will be there also, I hear.'

'And Hugh mac Ferdoragh of Dungannon,' added Hugh. 'Let you not forget him.'

'Could anyone overlook Hugh mac Ferdoragh? And what will they talk about, do you suppose?'

Hugh grinned. 'What do they ever talk about? The O'Neill will lay complaints against Hugh mac Ferdoragh. Hugh mac Ferdoragh will lay complaints against O'Neill. The Lord Deputy will take them both to task, and then demand again the rents and hostages he says he was promised out of Tír Chonaill. My father will beat his breast and promise to deliver them. Then they'll all go home and, sure, nobody will believe a word anyone is after saying.'

MacSweeney laughed. 'You have the truth of it, I'm thinking; and would you not like to be there yourself – to hear it all with your own ears?'

'And Perrot demanding hostages? I'd be the fool.'

'Ah, you would, you would.' His host nodded and swallowed a draught of wine. 'But it's more than petty squabbles, I'm thinking, is after drawing Sir John Perrot so far from the comforts of Dublin Castle.' He chuckled. 'Perhaps he and his English queen are after hearing all the rumours.'

'Rumours?'

'The old prophesy. Isn't it on everyone's lips again, and you out of your fosterage. *When Hugh succeeds Hugh, lawfully, lineally, and immediately, being formally and ceremoniously created according to the country's custom, the last Hugh shall be High King of all Ireland and drive all the foreigners out.'*

'High king, is it!' Hugh spluttered into his goblet. 'And wouldn't The O'Neill be having words to say on that score – and Hugh mac Ferdoragh. And what of the southern chieftains? Is Fiach mac Hugh the man to be laying his sword before a northern high king?'

'Or before any, if you go to that of it,' chuckled The MacSweeney, 'Fiach mac Hugh O'Byrne never had a mind to be ruled by anyone. But I am uneasy over this meeting. I don't trust the Lord Deputy. It is in my mind that the Saxons have their swords out for us.'

'But why? What are we after doing to anger them?'

'Apart from not paying our rents, you mean?'

'Well, that, to be sure, but, faith, they wouldn't go to war with us over a few cattle. They have been our friends – our allies against The O'Neill.'

'Ah, and there you come to the heart of the matter.' Donal was suddenly very serious. 'For I suspect it is not our allies they wish to be, but our masters. They have it in their minds to govern us, Hugh – to destroy our clan system, to abolish our Irish – Brehon – law and impose their own English customs in its place.'

'But that would be impossible!' Hugh stared at him. 'You can't destroy Brehon law. You might as well try to change the seasons or order a river to run uphill. It's what makes us who we are.'

'True,' said his host. 'But try telling that to Sir John

Perrot. The English don't have laws – only decrees and edicts. And they think what is right for them must be right for everyone.'

'But they never bothered us before.'

'They never feared us before.' He frowned. 'It is our friendship with Hugh mac Ferdoragh they distrust – and he married to your sister and like to be the next O'Neill when old Turlough Luineach finally drinks himself to death.' He shook his head. 'Think of it, Hugh. O'Donnell and O'Neill, the two greatest families in the land, united for the first time in living memory. No wonder Perrot is shouting for hostages.'

Hugh scowled. 'And he has a mind to betroth me to one of his daughters from his first marriage,' he said morosely, remembering a recent conversation he had not been meant to overhear.

'Who does? Perrot?'

'No, you great *amadán*, Hugh mac Ferdoragh.'

'Ah, does he now? Which daughter?'

'Does it make a difference?'

The MacSweeney chuckled. 'Speak for yourself, Hugh Roe, but were it myself they were marrying off, wouldn't I want to know who was to be sharing my bed?'

'But I don't want to be married off. Not till I'm at least –' Hugh projected his mind as far as he could imagine into the future '– till I'm at least thirty,' he finished decisively.

Donal MacSweeney roared with laughter. 'And how old are you now? Fourteen?'

'Fifteen – next month. And when – if – I ever marry, sure, it will be to a lass of my own choosing.'

'Then you had best keep yourself out of Hugh mac Ferdoragh's clutches.' The MacSweeney chuckled, clapping his young guest on the shoulder. 'Now, will I call my bards to entertain us, or do you have it in your mind to sit lecturing me all night?'

● ● ●

MacSweeney's bard took his place by the fire. Hugh sat with his chin in his hands staring into the dancing flames as he listened. The songs were old ones. They told of the Tuatha dé Danann – the ancient gods of Ireland: of the Dagda, keeper of the cauldron of plenty, whose prodigious appetite had once bought precious time for his people in their war against the Fomors. Of Lugh the sun god, of the hideous, red-haired Morrigu, the hag goddess of battles. They told of the great Manannán mac Lir, son of the sea and guardian of Ireland, who rode the waters in his chariot, 'the wave sweeper'. And lastly they sang of human affairs: tales of war, love – fulfilled or unrequited – battles and bravery and the high deeds of legendary heroes.

The notes fell from the harp like raindrops onto water – sometimes gentle, like the patter of a spring shower, sometimes loud and fierce as a winter storm. There was wind, too, in the music. It wept with the children of Lir, turned into swans by a cruel stepmother. It keened for Deirdre and the sons of Usnach. It howled round the ears of the legendary hero Finn mac Cumhaill and his warrior Fianna as they rode in pursuit of Finn's runaway wife, Gráinne, and her lover, Diarmuid.

Hugh closed his eyes and tried to imagine the Ireland of those songs. Where had it gone to? Where were the heroes of Ulster now, when she so needed them? His father was old and ruled by a woman. The O'Neill was a drunkard. Even the great Hugh mac Ferdoragh – he whom the English called Earl of Tyrone – wore English clothes, it was said, whenever he went to Dublin, and came to heel like an obedient hound when the Lord Deputy snapped his fingers.

Would the heroes of old have done such a shameful thing – King Conor mac Nessa of Ulster, or his champion the mighty Cúchulainn? And Conor's adversary – the fierce, bloodthirsty Queen Maeve of Connaught – would she have yielded her country to the old, red, English queen? Was I born too late, he wondered, as he made his way upstairs to bed. Has the hero-light died in the heart of Ireland?

He stood by the window and looked down for a moment at the sleeping lough. The waters were calm, peaceful in the moonlight – but they were dark, you couldn't see into them. And the little waves were restless. They sucked and slapped around the gunwales of the English ship and the noise of them was like the bubbling of the Dagda's cauldron – as if, somewhere beneath the surface of the lough, something alive was struggling to emerge.

two

THE FOLLOWING MORNING, The MacSweeney Fanad
dispatched a messenger to the *Matthew*, requesting wine
for his guests. The man returned, bringing the skipper,
Nicholas Barnes. Barnes had unwelcome news. 'The
wine merchant, Master Bermingham, is most sorry to dis-
oblige your honours,' he reported, 'but I am to tell you he
has sold all his wine and is preparing to sail.'

'What?' bellowed MacSweeney. 'And he after telling
me he had plenty for all comers?'

Barnes shook his head sympathetically. 'It is indeed
unfortunate,' he agreed. 'Master Bermingham had not
expected to sell his cargo so quickly. But what little we
have left is needed for the voyage home. The merchant
has asked me to convey his deepest apologies.'

'Apologies! What use, in the devil's name, are apologies and I with a houseful of guests? Isn't The
O'Donnell's son after riding all the way from Donegal to
buy wine for his father?'

'So I have learnt from your messenger. And Master

Bermingham would indeed be grieved to offend The O'Donnell or his son. He cannot sell wine to the young man, but he bids me say that if Hugh Roe and his companions would do him the honour of visiting our ship, he would be delighted to entertain them.'

MacSweeney refused to be mollified. 'The O'Donnell's son will consider your invitation,' he told Barnes coldly. 'But it is no joke to him to be coming all this way for nothing.'

Barnes made another eloquent gesture of apology and took his leave. The MacSweeney turned glumly to his guests. 'My sorrow,' he said. 'I am after offering what I could not supply.' He looked shattered and Hugh felt for him. To fail in hospitality was the greatest shame a chieftain could suffer.

'Don't be slighting yourself, Donal,' he urged. 'What journey could be for nothing and yourself at the end of it?'

The MacSweeney only shook his head. 'You are generous, Hugh Roe, but I promised you wine and I have none to give you. I am ashamed.'

'Ah, come on, man. How could you know the English merchant was a braggart and a liar?'

His words had little effect. Hugh hated to see his host so mortified. He looked at his companions – maybe they could help. Donal Gorm looked as glum as his father, but Eoghan O'Gallagher's face lit up wickedly. 'Cheer up,' he said, 'and I'll tell you what we'll do. We'll accept your man's invitation – all three of us. We'll visit his stinking ship and drink up every drop of wine he has left. We'll show that misbegotten son of a sow what it is to offend The MacSweeney Fanad.'

They all laughed. Even MacSweeney had to smile. 'And what if he does not offer you all he has?' he asked.

'How would he be refusing us – and we sitting in his own cabin and our tongues hanging out with the thirst?' Eoghan looked at his companions. 'Well, are you for coming with me?'

'I am, surely,' said Donal Gorm at once.

'And I,' agreed Hugh.

The MacSweeney looked doubtful. 'Well . . . I don't know. Wasn't the invitation really for Hugh Roe? – and himself a bit young I'm thinking to be downing all that wine.'

'I'll not have much, Donal,' promised Hugh, alarmed at the thought of spoiling everyone's fun. 'I'll drink very slowly, and the others will look after me, won't you?'

'Like hawks,' Donal Gorm assured his father; 'and he to do everything we tell him.'

'Well,' The MacSweeney relented, 'but mind you keep your word, now. Bring him home drunk and I'll tan your hides and make belts out of them.'

'Rest easy, Father,' promised Donal. 'We'll have him back sober as a friar.'

A local fisherman, one of MacSweeney's tenants, rowed them out to the ship in his little curragh that afternoon. 'Huroo, the *Matthew*,' bellowed Eoghan, as soon as they were within shouting distance. 'Hugh Roe O'Donnell has it in his mind to come aboard and sample your hospitality, and with him are the son of The MacSweeney Fanad, and the son of Eoghan O'Gallagher of Ballyshannon.'

The names must have sounded suitably impressive, for as the curragh came alongside, ladders were lowered and sailors helped the boys to scramble up onto the deck.

Nicholas Barnes received them effusively. 'It is indeed a privilege,' he purred, 'to welcome Sir Hugh O'Donnell's son and his friends aboard my ship. Master Bermingham will be honoured to entertain you and bids me say he has refreshments prepared for you in his cabin.'

He turned to lead the way aft. As the boys followed him, Hugh glanced around, puzzled. However great Master Bermingham's delight in their company, the merchant was clearly not planning to enjoy it for long. The others might not have noticed – too busy dreaming of Spanish sack, no doubt – but to Hugh it was obvious the vessel was being made ready to sail. There were men everywhere on the decks. Even Barnes seemed preoccupied. As he spoke to his guests, his eyes darted from side to side, checking the activity around him, and every now and then he was obliged to break off in the middle of a sentence to bellow orders to his crew. The sense of urgency made Hugh a little uneasy, though he could not have said why.

At the door of Bermingham's cabin, Barnes halted. 'Please to enter, your honours,' he said, throwing it open, 'and make yourselves at home.'

Eoghan and Donal obeyed eagerly, but Hugh hesitated for a moment. Turning, he looked back towards the

Fanad peninsula. In the sunshine, the lime-washed walls of Rathmullen Castle stood out sharply, white against the dark green of the surrounding forest. The tops of the trees quivered in a puff of air and, above them, an eagle soared on barely moving wings.

Hugh watched it, one hand shading his eyes. It quartered the sky patiently, till some movement below seemed to catch its eye. Then it dived deep into the trees like a tern plunging into water. After a moment it ascended again and beat away towards the west. Hugh followed its flight with envious eyes. Now, there was freedom! Would anyone give orders to eagles or tell them how to live their lives? He watched it till it was no more than a speck in the distance, then turned, half regretfully, and followed his friends into the cabin.

It was gloomy inside after the sunshine. The windows had been boarded up, as though against a storm, and that, too, was odd, for the water was calm and the sky blue and almost cloudless. The only source of light was a horn lantern swinging from a beam above the table.

Hugh blinked, trying to accustom his eyes to the shadow, and his unease heightened to a mild alarm. There was a wine flagon on the table, and Eoghan and Donal both had drinks in their hands, but of Bermingham or his promised feast there was no sign. He took a step forward then hesitated. The door shut behind him with a solid clunk, blotting out the last chink of natural light. He spun round and heard a key turn in the lock.

'*Dhia*!' Frantically, he flung himself at the door,

rattling the handle. Nothing happened. He hammered and kicked at the wood and yelled with all his strength. 'Let me out! Open the door, you swine! Let me out!'

The others stared at him. 'What the devil is on you, Hugh Roe?' asked Eoghan O'Gallagher.

'They're after locking us in.'

'What?' They rushed over and added their weight to his own, hurling themselves repeatedly against the door. But the timbers were solid oak – they didn't give an inch. They tried to prize open the windows, but Barnes and Bermingham had been thorough and those boards had been designed to withstand the fury of Atlantic gales.

They were trapped.

On the deck outside, the sounds of activity rose to a crescendo. There was an ominous creaking noise as the anchor cable started to come in. The boys listened to it, their hearts cold with fear. 'What are they doing to us?' whispered Hugh. No one answered him.

Snatches of conversation echoed in his mind. *'Would you not like to be there yourself – to hear it all with your own ears?'*

'And Perrot demanding hostages? I'd be the fool.' Chre-esta, but wasn't he though? – a blind, trusting fool who had walked, simple as a calf, into the trap laid by Perrot's oily-tongued agents. How they must be laughing up there on deck – Barnes and that merchant Bermingham. Anger and frustration boiled up inside him and he hurled himself at the door again, hammering on the wood and screaming abuse at his captors till his voice cracked and

his knuckles were raw and bleeding.

In the end Eoghan dragged him forcibly away and thrust him into a seat with a beaker of wine in his hand. 'Will you shut your gob and get that into you,' he said. 'You'll help no one and you acting like a madman.'

Hugh took a long gulp and looked about him more steadily. He felt the ship swing round and begin to make way.

'She's going up the lough,' said Donal, lifting his head and calculating. 'She has the full of her sails of wind and it blowing from the south-east.'

'Then we'll be beating into it all the way to Dublin,' said Eoghan grimly.

He lapsed into silence and the others retreated into their own gloom. There was really nothing to talk about, and one flagon of wine between the three of them was not sufficient to dull their misery.

For half an hour or so they sat in silence, then Hugh heard footsteps outside the cabin. A key turned, the door opened. The man standing in the doorway had to be the merchant, John Bermingham. The bland face and pudgy hands suggested money and soft living. The man's dress was extraordinary – though probably the height of English fashion – a short, ermine-trimmed cloak, a heavily embroidered velvet doublet and a pair of trunk hose so short and padded they made him look as though he had crammed his backside into a giant puffball.

Hugh stared at him. Despite everything, it was all he could do not to laugh. How did the man ever manage to sit down in such a ridiculous outfit? Bermingham, however, appeared to have no idea how absurd he looked. He beamed at his captives as though delighted with his own treachery. 'So. Three fine birds in one net. And you . . .' here he looked pointedly at Hugh's red locks, 'you must be O'Donnell's son – the one they call Red Hugh.'

He smirked, as though he had accomplished some great feat of deduction. Hugh itched to wipe the smile off his face. 'I am Hugh Roe O'Donnell,' he acknowledged haughtily, 'and I demand to be put ashore immediately.'

'Ah, do you now?' The smirk became a positive leer. 'Such pride and arrogance in one so young. But I fear, my young fighting cock, you are no longer in a position to demand anything. You are my prisoner. The queen herself has commanded –'

'A pox on your queen, and she a howling old hag of a woman! What right has she to be giving orders to the son of O'Donnell?'

'What right?' Bermingham's face was a study in shock and astonishment. 'Why, how dare you speak so against Her Majesty? How dare you insult your . . . your . . .' he groped for a suitably imposing Irish title – 'your lawful Árd Rí.'

'High king, is it? The devil mend you for a liar! I have no high king.'

'Of course you have – the queen's grace is –'

'Is nothing to me. O'Donnell is my chieftain. I will serve no other. I spit on your English queen!' And he demonstrated.

'You filthy little animal!' The merchant's fat belly quivered with rage. He lunged forward and Hugh, snatching up the wine flagon, flung it at his head. It caught the man flush on the nose. He staggered backwards, his hands clutched to his face, and before he could recover, Hugh dived though the doorway and made a wild dash for the side of the ship. It was madness – he knew it. The deck was high, they were a long way from shore. If he didn't break his neck he would probably drown. But better that than . . .

He should have realised, of course. He should have guessed Bermingham would not come unattended. There were half a dozen men outside the door and though his charge took them by surprise, he was not halfway across the deck before they caught him. He kicked and fought and scratched like a cornered fox but they dragged him back to the cabin and threw him down, held him on his knees at Bermingham's feet.

Bermingham looked down at him. The merchant's nose was swollen like a piece of bread dough. It dripped blood all down his fancy clothes. He took his belt off and wound the buckle end slowly round his soft, white hand.

'You may think yourself of great account here in the north, Master O'Donnell,' he said in a choking voice, 'but, by the mass, we'll teach you some humility in Dublin.' And he raised his arm and slashed the belt down across Hugh's face.

The leather bit like a branding iron. Hugh gasped and struggled wildly, but his captors twisted his arms behind his back and seized fistfuls of his hair to prevent him from moving. Bermingham raised his arm again. His eyes glittered, little muscles twitched along his jaws and his tongue slithered over his lips like a fat, pink lizard. Hugh watched him helplessly.

The arm flicked. The thong sliced down again – searing, slashing, over and over, until at last Hugh screamed. Only then did the merchant seem satisfied. 'And that's only the start,' he warned, re-clasping the buckle around his paunch. 'Cross me again and I'll make you wish you'd never been born.' He barked something in English to his men, and then repeated it in Irish for the benefit of his prisoners. 'Take them below and put them in irons. And if they give you any trouble, thrash them.'

They sat in darkness, somewhere in the bowels of the ship. Pain and shock gnawed like rats at Hugh's mind. 'That's only the start,' Bermingham had said. What lay in wait for him in Dublin? Would they torture him? Were the dungeons as black as rumour reported them? Would he spend the rest of his life chained like an animal in cold and darkness? Oh, God, he thought. He hunched himself into a tight ball and a small sound escaped his throat.

Someone moved in the darkness. 'Hugh?' said Donal's voice. 'Hugh, are you all right there?'

'The little bit that's left of me.' He tried to make a joke of it, but his voice didn't sound right, even to him.

'Misbegotten Saxon swine!' said Eoghan O'Gallagher. There was a rattling sound as he struggled with his manacles.

Hugh felt a wave of guilt. It's all my fault, he thought, for insulting Bermingham and breaking his nose. 'I'm sorry,' he said aloud. 'It's my dirty temper that's after putting us all down here.'

Eoghan chuckled. 'Ah, but did you see the face on him?' he gloated, 'and him bleeding like a stuck pig. Doesn't it do your heart good to be thinking about it?'

He laughed, and Donal with him, but Hugh could not even raise a smile. He lifted manacled hands to touch his swollen face. What comfort was revenge in a situation like this? It was like a nightmare – only you woke from nightmares. This horror might go on forever. He might rot and die in a lightless dungeon below the walls of Dublin Castle.

Was this a punishment? He thought of his sins – his pride, his willfulness. I'm sorry, he wanted to plead, I didn't mean it. I'll marry the oldest and ugliest daughter Hugh mac Ferdoragh has. I'll put my foot on the inauguration stone tomorrow; I'll rule all Ulster for you and you wishing it. Only, please, please, make this terrible thing not be happening.

But there was no one to say it to, no one to forgive him, no one to wind back time and let him start again. There was only the darkness, the fetid stench of the hold, and the cold iron around his wrists and ankles.

The hours dragged by. Eoghan and Donal talked listlessly. Hugh sat in silence fighting back fear and nausea. The *Matthew* had reached the open sea and was lifting and dropping with gut-wrenching monotony.

'Eoghan,' Hugh asked at last – anything to take his mind off his misery – 'Eoghan, you saw him once? What is he like, this John Perrot?'

'A bull,' said Eoghan grimly. 'A great, hulking bull with an ugly face and a temper to match. They say he is old King Harry's illegitimate son – half-brother to the English queen – but it is not the Saxon way to be recognising bastards, so she sends him over here to keep him out of her way.'

'No wonder he's bad-tempered,' said Donal, and he laughed, but it was a hollow sound.

Hugh shuddered. Be strong, he told himself. You are a chieftain's son. But it was hard to be brave in total darkness, weaponless and in chains. If he had a sword, or a knife – anything with which to defend himself. He thought about stories he had heard of men who had fought without weapons, bards who had destroyed their enemies with satire, stinging them to death with cruel and biting wit. Was such a thing possible? He was no bard, but he had a tongue in his head and he knew how to use it.

Comforted a little, he finally fell asleep, but his dreams were fitful and he woke feeling more nauseous than ever. The hold was foul – it stank of tar and bilge water and rotting wood. He was sweating despite the cold, his forehead felt damp and clammy and he began to yawn uncontrollably.

'I'm hungry,' complained Eoghan suddenly. 'Are they going to feed us, do you suppose, on this damn voyage?'

'Hungry?' said Donal's voice incredulously. 'Sure, it's a stomach like an old billy goat you must have, O'Gallagher! I couldn't touch food at this moment and you providing it. What about yourself, Hugh?'

Food! At the very thought of it, Hugh's diaphragm fluttered and his throat muscles went into spasm. 'Oh, *Chreesta*,' he gasped, and he threw up violently.

three

'THE *MATTHEW* HAS docked, my Lord,' announced a secretary. 'They are bringing the prisoners up to the castle
now.'

'Excellent,' said the Lord Deputy. 'Inform the constable, and tell him to see them lodged in the gate-tower –
except O'Donnell's son. Have him brought to the castle
chamber, I wish to question him.'

'Very good, my Lord.'

The secretary withdrew. Sir John Perrot rubbed his
hands and smiled. At last, he thought. This would silence
the wolves snapping at his heels. He knew of the plots
against him, the whispered tales carried back to the Privy
Council in London. Well, let them intrigue – this time, he
had outwitted them. In a daring coup, he had taken into
his keeping the best hostages out of all Tír Chonaill. The
O'Donnell and that Scottish harridan of a wife of his could
now be brought to heel. The queen would acknowledge
his statesmanship, and Dublin would be obliged to follow
suit. Oh, how his enemies on the Council would squirm.

They would puke with envy and he would rub their noses in it. He smoothed his ruff, settled the lace at his cuffs and made his way down to the castle chamber.

Stephen Seagar, the Constable of Dublin Castle, escorted the prisoner in. 'Master O'Donnell, my Lords,' he announced, thrusting into the room a bundle of rags that looked – and smelt – as if it had been plucked off the nearest dunghill.

The company stared and dabbed scented handkerchiefs to their noses. Perrot blinked in amazement. There must be some mistake. Could this creature really be Hugh Roe O'Donnell, the golden child around whom those ridiculous prophecies had been spun? It looked more like a drowned rat, fished out of a cesspit.

He sighed. One forgot sometimes, here in Dublin, how savage the untamed Irish really were. Scratch any one of their so-called princes and you'd find a fleabitten wolf underneath. 'Faugh!' he said disgustedly. 'He stinks like a polecat.'

'He has been confined for several days in the hold of a ship, my Lord,' one of his Councillors, Sir Lucas Dillon, pointed out reasonably. 'In chains . . . and probably seasick.'

'Hmph!' Perrot was unconvinced. Dillon was his friend – indeed, his chief stay on the Council – but he had Irish blood. He probably felt compelled to defend this little animal. Perrot knew better. He could not imagine any English gentleman allowing himself to sink into that state, no matter what the circumstances.

Wrinkling his nose, he moved forward to inspect his catch more closely. The brat had his head down and was wrapped from head to foot in one of those barbaric Irish mantles. All Perrot could see of him was a tangle of red hair and one thin hand that had crept out to hold the edges of his cloak together. He was shivering, but whether from fear or cold, it was impossible to tell.

After a moment the boy looked up. His other hand came out from his cloak and scraped the matted hair from his eyes. For the first time Perrot saw his face. God's death! The little guttersnipe had been brawling, too. His left eye was swollen shut and both cheeks were a mass of welts and bruises.

Clearly, there could be little intelligence in such a creature. 'I bid you good day, Master O'Donnell,' Perrot said brusquely. 'I am sorry your father's intransigence has obliged us to bring you here by force.'

The silent figure gave no indication of having understood or even heard his words. Lucas Dillon translated them into Irish. The boy looked at Dillon. He seemed to be thinking. Then he looked at Perrot. He fixed the Lord Deputy with his one good eye and said clearly and carefully: 'And that is the first lie. You have neither sorrow nor shame. You rejoice in your perfidy.'

Latin! The disgusting little animal spoke perfect Latin – the result, no doubt of a Popish education. Perrot thought rapidly. He would have to pick his words with care. It was entirely possible the little savage spoke the language better than he did, but Perrot could hardly insist that Lucas Dillon translate everything. He hesitated a long time before speaking again. 'It ill becomes you,' he said at last in Latin, 'to speak of perfidy, Master O'Donnell, when I have it on good authority that your own father is planning to disinherit his eldest son – who has done him no wrong that I ever heard of – in order to make you his heir.'

The boy looked baffled. 'You speak in riddles,' he said.

'Have you not an older brother?'

'A half-brother. What of it?'

'By law he stands before you in line of succession.'

'By whose law?'

'By English law; by the law of all civilised kingdoms.'

The boy laughed softly. 'A foolish law indeed, my Lord Deputy, that disinherits strong men and gives power to women and weaklings. Our Brehon law gives authority to the ablest man.' He paused and looked Perrot full in the face. 'Even bastards.'

Perrot felt every eye in the room turn to look at him. His prisoner smiled. Perrot wanted to wipe the insolence off his face. He restrained himself with an effort. 'And what does that accomplish,' he asked coldly, 'but to set every man within bowshot of the title against his rivals. Uncle against nephew, cousin against cousin – why, men murder their own brothers over your Gaelic titles.'

'But they do not execute their wives,' said Hugh Roe O'Donnell softly. 'Two, wasn't it? Anne Boleyn? Catherine Howard?'

It was too much. John Perrot, bastard son of King Henry VIII, roared like a baited bull and swung a blow calculated to snap the boy's neck. But Lucas Dillon stepped in at the last minute. 'Let it go,' he urged, seizing the enraged man by the arm. 'The boy is angry and exhausted. He does not know what he is saying.'

But it was obvious the brat knew exactly what he was saying. He stood there wrapped in his filthy blanket and stared at the Lord Deputy with all the arrogance of an emperor. Perrot struggled with his rage. He choked on it, gurgling like a man cut living from the gallows. His fists clenched and unclenched convulsively.

At last, with a supreme effort, he mastered himself. 'Out,' he roared. 'Take him from my sight before I kill him.'

Seagar didn't wait to be told twice. He seized his prisoner by the shoulders and propelled him towards the door. The boy twisted in his grasp and lifted his head to hurl a parting insult, but Seagar clapped a hand over his mouth and shoved him through the door before he could speak.

✦ ✦ ✦

'Ah, didn't you tell him, though,' chuckled Eoghan O'Gallagher, still gloating two weeks later over the perceived humiliation of their captor. 'And him with his pride all over him like muck on a pig's back.'

Hugh sighed. Eoghan's way of coping with captivity seemed to be to treat it like a game – a verbal hurling match, with every insult a goal for the Irish side. But Eoghan had not confronted the Lord Deputy. Hugh knew the truth. They were powerless – Perrot could do whatever he liked with them. His own bravado in the castle chamber had been no more than the courage of a mouse, squeaking insults from between the jaws of a cat.

He stood up restlessly and went to look out the window. At least, so far, they had been spared the underground dungeon of his nightmares. They were housed in a room at the top of the gate-tower and though they were locked in for much of the time, it was a pleasant enough prison, decently furnished and with windows, overlooking the bridge.

From his perch on the windowsill, Hugh looked north towards the River Liffey to watch the comings and goings between the castle and the wharves. He had never seen a large town before and if they were all like Dublin he never wanted to see another. It was so dirty. The streets were grey, the houses were grey, even the sky seemed permanently overcast, and the breeze blowing off the river carried with it the stench of the wharves – a mixture of fish and sewage and rotting vegetables.

There was another smell also, when the wind was in the right direction. None of the boys ever spoke of it, but they knew what it was. On the way up from the ship, Seagar had pointed out to them the spikes above the castle gate and the trophies impaled on them – the grinning, sightless heads rotting in the weather. Irish heads, the Constable had told them – a warning to any would-be rebels of the fate that befell all traitors to the crown.

Today the wind was in the east so they were spared the lesson. Hugh shivered. 'It's raining again,' he said, peering down.

Eoghan laughed. 'And why wouldn't it? Even the sky spits on Englishmen.'

'But does it have to spit on us as well? They'll not let us into the yards today, and it raining.'

Eoghan shrugged. He lifted a playing piece from the board on the table and plonked it down again triumphantly. 'There, get out of that, Donal – if you can.'

His voice almost cracked with glee, and, despite himself, Hugh felt his interest rising. He had yet to see Donal lose a game of *ficheall*. He slid from the window seat and came over to watch. Donal frowned. He studied the board for a moment, then reached out and shifted one of his own pieces. 'You spoke too soon, Eoghan,' he said quietly. 'Two moves there are open to you now – and you a dead man whichever way you jump.'

'Nonsense!' Eoghan's hand shot out confidently, but then faltered and hovered uncertainly above the board.

Donal chuckled.

'Ah, to hell with it for a stupid game, anyway,' said Eoghan. He pushed his chair back from the table and stood up. 'Where's the skill in pushing counters round a board?'

'You are too fiery, Eoghan,' Donal told him. 'You rush into battle without studying the field and doesn't it bring you down every time?'

Eoghan snorted and muttered something uncompli-
mentary, but his friend only laughed. 'You'll learn,' he
said. He held the pieces out to Hugh. 'Will you try your
hand, Hugh Roe.'

Hugh shook his head. In the mood he was in, he
would be no match for Donal. He wished he had the
young MacSweeney's temperament. Donal had adapted
to captivity better than any of them.

He went back to the window. Donal cleared the
board and set himself up a practice game. Eoghan paced
the floor. 'I'm sick of this damn room,' he exploded.

As if on cue there was a knock at the door. They
looked at one another hopefully. It must be a visitor, for
which of their jailers ever bothered to knock? 'Come in,'
said Hugh, and the door opened to admit Sir Lucas Dillon.

Dillon had visited them several times, and Hugh and
Donal, at least, were always pleased to see him. He was
one of the few men about the castle who seemed to have
any concern for their welfare. He smiled at the boys. 'I
came to see are they still treating you decently,' he said.

'They're feeding us,' growled Eoghan.

'Are they now? Then let you be thankful for small
mercies. Is there anything you need?'

'We need our freedom.'

'My sorrow, but that is the one thing I cannot give
you. However,' the man put down a pile of books, 'I
thought these might help to pass the time.'

Hugh pounced on them and thumbed through them

eagerly. 'But they're all written in English,' he said in disappointment, 'and we have no English – any of us.'

Dillon looked at him sideways. 'Then perhaps it might pay you to learn.'

'The devil, it might!' spluttered Eoghan. 'Is it ourselves to be aping English ways?'

Dillon smiled. 'I know it's little liking you have for the English, but would it not make sense – and you living among them – to learn their language?'

'It would not! I'd rather be dead!'

'And so you may be, and you not learning to curb your tongue.' Dillon sighed patiently. 'Can you not understand, lad, times are changing. The old ways, the old customs, they are dying – slowly perhaps, but the end is inevitable. England has strength and patience. Eventually she will win.'

His words went through Hugh like a knife. What was it Donal's father had said? '*They have it in their minds to govern us, Hugh – to destroy the clan system, to abolish Brehon law and impose their own English laws in its place.*' He shivered, as if an icy wind had blown through the room. Looking up, he saw Lucas Dillon watching him. There was sympathy in the man's face but it did not comfort him.

Eoghan seethed with indignation. 'She will not win,' he said fiercely. 'We will fight her every step of the way.'

'So you will,' said Dillon, sadly, 'when you are not too busy fighting each other. You are your own worst enemies, and that is the sorrow of it. You are too proud to be led, and because you will not have an Irish king, in the end, you will have to submit to an English queen.'

'Ha! – and she to be bending her own knee to the King of Spain before the next year is out.'

'What did you say?' Dillon rounded on the boy, his face white with shock. 'You little idiot! Don't you ever utter such words again and you wanting to keep your head on your shoulders.'

Eoghan looked startled, but he scowled unrepentantly. 'And is it not what everyone is saying – that King Philip is even now fitting out an Armada to blow your navy off the seas?'

'They don't say it here,' said Dillon grimly, 'and no more will you and you having the sense you were born with. Why, if the Council believed you had the slightest inkling of any Spanish plot . . .'

Hugh and Donal stared at each other solemnly.

'He'll not speak of it again,' promised Hugh. 'He is not a fool, for all that he has a big mouth.'

'See that he doesn't,' said Dillon. 'For if they decide to question him I'll not be able to save him.' He looked hard at Eoghan. 'You understand what I'm saying to you?'

Eoghan muttered under his breath.

'Answer me!'

'Ah, all right, then, I do.'

'Then let you not forget it.'

Eoghan remained subdued for some weeks after Dillon's visit – obviously the warning had shaken him more than he would admit. They had all heard tales of the interrogations that took place in the castle dungeons. Eventually, however, his irrepressible optimism got the better of him.

The Spanish rumours had refused to go away, and if Sir Lucas Dillon was unwilling to discuss them, there were others less reluctant. Stories jumped like fleas around the castle yards and, like fleas, they fattened on every man who carried them. Eoghan carried all of them – back to the safety of the gate-tower after each exercise period, to be repeated in gleeful whispers after the guards had barred the door and departed for the night.

The months passed. Christmas came and went, winter gave way to spring, and the whispers grew to an alarming rumble. Five hundred ships, they asserted; a thousand, two thousand – the greatest Armada ever assembled. They had left Cadiz, they were at Corunna, they had set sail for the English coast.

'They are coming like Finn and his Fianna,' crowed the Irish horseboys, 'to help the Irish in their hour of need.'

'They are swarming like the hordes of hell,' muttered the English soldiers, 'with orders from the Pope to destroy the English nation. They carry racks and thumbscrews in their holds, and nooses to hang Godfearing Protestants.'

By May the castle was in a frenzy. Everyone told a different story and everyone claimed to have the truth of it. Hugh didn't know what to believe. Conflict seemed certain – the fear on the garrison was something you could almost smell. But whether the news was as good as the rumours suggested was another matter entirely. Donal treated the stories with scepticism. But Eoghan refused to entertain doubts. 'We'll be out of here by Christmas,' he insisted repeatedly, 'and a row of ugly English heads grinning down on us from the spikes over the gate as we go.'

'And the pity of it that Perrot's will not be one of them,' said Donal, dryly. He winked at Hugh. 'My soul, hasn't he the luck on him, and him being recalled now to England, and leaving next month.'

'The new Lord Deputy will look well enough in his place,' retorted Eoghan, 'and, sure there are spikes enough in London for Sir John Perrot. They can stick him up beside his red witch of a sister, and we'll all go over and throw mud at them.'

Hugh and Donal could only look at each other and shake their heads. 'Well, I'll tell you this for nothing,' said Donal with a chuckle. 'If the Spanish do come here, they'll not want to be landing in the west. For if the rocks and tides don't get them, sure, the O'Malleys will.'

FOUR

PERROT'S APPROACHING DEPARTURE brought a rush of activity to the castle. The retiring Lord Deputy was determined, it seemed, to go out in a blaze of glory. Countless farewell pageants were contrived for him – and largely by him – and the road between the wharves and the gate-towers became choked with well-wishers arriving to pay their respects. Hugh and his friends, watching the daily comings and goings from their prison window, were not deceived by all the seeming goodwill. 'Well-wishers, is it?' scoffed Donal. 'And Dublin Castle bulging at the seams with all their hostages. Your man would do anything to impress his sister. Even Fiach mac Hugh is after receiving a safe conduct, I hear.'

'And three of his sons in Perrot's hands to make sure he accepts it,' added Hugh bitterly. 'Well, I'll tell you this for nothing. The English queen may believe this show of duty, but it will not fool anyone here. The only Irishman who'll shed unforced tears for Sir John Perrot is old Tur-lough Luineach – and, sure he'd weep at parting company with his own spittle, and he in his cups.'

They all laughed. 'Ah well,' said Donal philosophi-
cally. 'At least your father will be here, Hugh Roe, and
you having the chance to see him.'

Hugh frowned. Donal was right, but there was one
thing he seemed to have forgotten. The O'Donnell would
come to Dublin no more willingly than Fiach mac Hugh
O'Byrne. He, Hugh Roe, would be the knife held to his
father's throat and that knowledge was a bitter draught to
swallow.

He blamed himself also for the current turmoil in Tír
Chonaill. Visitors to Dublin reported that, since his
abduction, the ambitions of his father's would-be successors had erupted into violence again. One of the
claimants, Hugh mac Calvagh, had apparently allied himself with The O'Neill to inflict a crushing military defeat
on O'Donnell and his ally, Hugh mac Ferdoragh. The
pretender had not survived long enough to profit from his
victory, but in the meantime The O'Donnell's uncle,
Hugh mac Hugh Dubh, and nephew Niall Garbh were
both rattling their own swords, and Donnell O'Donnell
was quietly gathering supporters and awaiting his opportunity. The country was dissolving into anarchy, and
under cover of the confusion, a rabble of English soldiery
had sacked Donegal Friary and installed themselves in its
cloisters.

Hugh had happy memories of Donegal Friary – he
had heard mass in its chapel, stolen apples from its
orchards, received religious instruction from its Guardian,

Brother Tadhg O'Boyle. To think of it now, desecrated by drunken heretics, its occupants slain or scattered God knew where, was a pain almost beyond bearing. Time and again he cursed himself for the naïve idiot he had been at Rathmullen.

● ● ●

The O'Donnell and his wife rode into Dublin one afternoon in mid-May. They were given lodgings in the castle, and the following morning Hugh was brought to their apartments to visit them. It was an uncomfortable reunion. He looked at his father – so visibly aged in the short time since last they had been together – at his angry, tight-lipped mother, and did not know what to say. Is it me she is angry at? he wondered. Does she blame me for this mess?

To make matters worse, his parents were not alone, and when Hugh saw who the other visitor was, his heart sank even further. Hugh mac Ferdoragh O'Neill! Hugh had never felt easy in this man's presence. There was something too subtle, too *unIrish*, about him – and it was not simply his English title, Earl of Tyrone. Hugh mac Ferdoragh was a secretive man. He thought much and spoke little, which made it difficult to read his mind, and Hugh Roe was not used to such restraint. The Iníon Dubh never left anyone in doubt as to her feelings – she was renowned for her rages. The O'Donnell did not mince his words either. And when Eoghan's father – or Donal's – lost his temper the whole world knew about it.

But Hugh mac Ferdoragh smiled and dissembled. He seldom raised his voice. The man who crossed him might never realise his mistake till he felt the knife between his ribs. In his presence, Hugh had always felt very young and inadequate.

He sensed the man's gaze on him now, and tried to ignore it as he walked forward to greet his father. The O'Donnell held his hands out. 'Ah Hugh, ah, son, isn't it grand to see you again.'

His voice was an old man's. Hugh could not answer. Shame and guilt strangled the words in his throat. He clasped the old man's hands and kissed him on the cheek as duty allowed. His eyes sought his mother. Help me, he begged silently. Support me, forgive me, or I am done for.

Tall and imposing as the Morrigu, the Iníon Dubh regarded her son in silence. Then, suddenly, she too held out her arms and her fierceness dissolved into a loving smile. 'No shame to you, my Hugh Roe,' she said softly. 'Aren't we all after being deceived by English treachery?'

His defences crumbled. Pride, shame, dignity dissolved like icicles in rain. He went into her arms and wept there like a child.

Nobody jeered, nobody censured him. And afterwards, words came more easily. Fear for himself turned into concern for her own safety. 'You should not be here,' he told her. 'It's not safe for you here, not after . . . '

She chuckled. 'You mean after what happened Hugh mac Calvagh? They told you of that, did they?'

He nodded.

His mother shrugged. 'Ah, well. And little enough there was to tell, if you go to that of it. He died. He came to Mongavlin after the battle, boasting of his victory, and died there in a drunken brawl.'

'The English say it was murder – and you after ordering it.'

'He was their creature – it pleases them to believe so. Hugh mac Calvagh was a traitor who took arms against his chieftain. He paid the price for it.'

She made it sound simple but he knew better. 'And what defence will that be?' he demanded, 'once the English are after arresting you?'

'They'll not arrest me. I have the personal assurance of the Lord Deputy.'

'The word of an Englishman?'

They all laughed, But it was Hugh mac Ferdoragh who answered him. 'You are learning fast, Hugh Roe,' he said approvingly. 'But bear in mind, your mother is not the only one here under a guarantee of safe conduct. How would Fiach mac Hugh take it, do you think, if Perrot were to go back on his word? I'll tell you. He would be away to the mountains as fast as his horse could carry him, and every other chieftain who valued his skin hot on his heels.' He chuckled. 'And then who would be left to line the banks of the Liffey and give the old fool his grand farewell?'

Hugh had to smile. 'All the same though . . .'

'Forget it,' said his mother, shaking her head. 'It is over – done with – one less dog to bay at The O'Donnell's heels.'

'But there will be others.'

'And they all going the same way!'

Her confidence was inspiring. But suddenly Hugh remembered his own impotence. Anger rose like a wave inside him. 'I should be with you,' he raged. 'I should be leading your army.'

'And so you will be. Have patience, my son. They cannot keep you here for ever.'

But they could – and she knew it as well as he did. He looked down a long, dark tunnel into the future. 'They have me like a fly in a spider's web,' he said bitterly, 'and they'll not let me go till they are after sucking the life from me.'

'Stop it!' The Iníon Dubh gripped him by the shoulders and shook him hard. 'Stop it at once! Is it a child you are to be talking this foolish way?'

'We are not after deserting you, Hugh,' put in Hugh mac Ferdoragh. 'There are ways out of this castle – and I not without the friends and resources to find them.'

'And they trying and failing once already. Didn't Perrot boast to me himself that you were after offering him a thousand pounds for my escape, and he refusing you.'

'He had the truth of it,' the man admitted. 'But Perrot is a wealthy man with little need of my money, and frightened half to death of that harridan of a sister of his. The incoming Lord Deputy, God rot his soul, is another mess of pottage entirely. Sir William Fitzwilliam.' His mouth twitched into a sneer. 'We had him once before – he was greedy then and I'll wager he is greedy still. A weasel doesn't change its nature. Give him time to settle in and we'll see what a little tickle on his palm will do. Meanwhile, let you not think he is the only horse in my stable. I am already after writing to Lord Burghley and Sir Francis Walsingham. They are influential men – Privy Councillors, both of them – and both owing me favours.'

Hugh felt ashamed. 'I'm sorry,' he said. 'You are doing your best. It is not my place to be complaining. Only . . .' He sighed. How could he explain what it was like to spend your days shut away behind high walls, to watch the world pass you by through one small window, to depend on your captors for the most basic necessities. 'Sometimes,' he said, 'I am hard-pressed not to beat my brains out against the wall.'

'I understand,' said Hugh mac Ferdoragh. 'Prison is hard for any man and you are very young. But have faith in me. I will plead for you, lie for you – anything it takes. Sure, didn't I even tell Walsingham you were my son-in-law? I need you free, Hugh Roe. Tír Chonaill needs you free. And we will not fail you. Let you trust in that.'

Hugh blinked. That must be the most impassioned speech he had ever heard the man make. But what did it mean? He could understand his importance to Tír Chonaill but why would Hugh mac Ferdoragh need him so badly? He searched his mind for a glimmer of understanding. The chieftaincy? The O'Neill title? Of course, that was it. For Hugh mac Ferdoragh to set his own foot on the inauguration stone when Turlough Luineach died, he would need all the backing he could muster. A strong –

and friendly – Tír Chonaill would be crucial to his success. Wasn't it for that the man was after marrying one of O'Donnell's daughters? It explained something else too.

'Did you really tell Walsingham I was your son-in-law?' he asked the would-be O'Neill curiously.

'I did,' admitted his champion.

'And which of your daughters am I supposed to be after marrying?'

'Well, let me see now.' The man put his head to one side and pretended to consider the matter carefully. 'I've not many left now, you'll mind, and they unmarried, but Róis is about your age. On consideration, sure, I think you'd do very well together.'

'And . . .' Hugh was almost speechless. '. . . and Róis? What has Róis to say about all this?'

'Ah, well, now,' Hugh mac Ferdoragh tipped him a broad wink. 'Won't you have to ask her that yourself?'

The next six weeks passed quickly. Sir John Perrot was fêted and flattered by his guests. He made a pompous speech to the hostages, telling them how fortunate they were to be locked up in Dublin Castle where none could accuse them of sedition; and finally he sailed off down the Liffey to the cheers and tears of a large crowd. The cheers were universal, but whether from appreciation or relief nobody would say. The tears were supplied by Turlough Luineach. 'And he so full of wine, wasn't it running out of him at both ends?' observed the Iníon Dubh, waspishly, describing the pageant to her son. Hugh could imagine it. He was glad he had been spared the sight.

At last the time came for their final meeting. With Perrot gone, the Iníon Dubh no longer felt safe in Dublin. Hugh had not realised how much this leavetaking would affect him, but as he kissed his mother farewell he felt an overwhelming surge of homesickness. They were going home – back to the mountains, the salmon streams, the green, forest places of Tír Chonaill, and he must remain here imprisoned like an eagle in a cage.

He struggled to keep his feelings hidden, but there was no deceiving the Iníon Dubh. She put her hands on his shoulders. 'Courage, Hugh Roe. Have faith in us. We will not fail you. Whatever it takes, whatever it may cost, there is nothing we will leave undone and it serving to bring you home again.'

He carried her words back to the gate-house and tried to believe in them as he sat on the windowsill and watched the rain.

Five

LIKE A WOUNDED albatross, driven before the wind, the *Trinidad Valencera* battled her way round the northern coastline of Tír Chonaill. Apart from the sheer bulk of her, there was little left to show that she had once been the pride of the Levantine Squadron in the greatest Armada that Spain or any other country in the world had ever assembled. That glorious dream was over – shattered in one battle off the coast of France – and the southerly winds which had saved the *Trinidad Valencera* from the Dunkirk shoals had not, in the end, proved kind to her. Driven northward and unable to regain the channel passage, she had been forced to set a course around the top of Scotland. Now the autumn gales of the North Atlantic were completing the work begun by English cannons. Her sails were shredded, her rigging damaged. And she had lost her heaviest anchors – cut them and run on that terrible night off Calais when Drake's fireships had come sailing out of the darkness on the flood tide, spitting flames like a pride of vengeful dragons.

Below decks, she was a floating pesthouse. There was no food. What little water remained lay in green and putrid pools in the bottoms of barrels. Her crew was dying. More than five hundred men – her own and those rescued from the sinking *Barco de Amburgo* – lay crammed together in a space designed for less than a quarter of that number. They were starving, half-crazed with thirst and suffering from wounds, scurvy and dysentery. Soon they would all be too weak to man the pumps or take their turn at the steerage.

'Take great heed lest you fall upon the Island of Ireland,' their commander, the Duke of Medina Sidonia, had warned his captains, 'for fear of the harm that may happen unto you upon that coast.'

But the *Trinidad Valencera* had no choice. With her canvas torn and spars shattered, she could do nothing but run before the sou'westerlies. Besides, if she did not find food and clean water her crew would be dead long before she reached the coast of Spain. Wallowing in the Atlantic swell and listing more dangerously with every hour that passed, she ploughed through Inishtrahull Sound and eastward along the coast of Inishowen until, finally, she dropped her remaining anchors in Glenagivney Bay.

❉ ❉ ❉

'Your position is hopeless,' declared Henry Hovenden. 'Your ship is wrecked. Your men are dying. You have nowhere to go. Surrender to me and I will conduct you safely to Dublin and see that you are sent to London to plead your case.'

Colonel Alonzo de Luzon swayed on his feet and considered the offer. What the Englishman said was true. The *Trinidad Valencera* had finally broken up in Glenagivney Bay and he and his wretched band of survivors had been on the road for twelve days since, looking for food and shelter. They would be no match for Hovenden's private army. But . . . surrender? He was an officer in the army of his most Catholic Majesty, King Philip of Spain – and these starving men were his responsibility. He had heard stories of how the English treated their prisoners.

'Your soldiers are hungry,' pressed the Englishman, as if reading his mind, 'and exhausted. You have come far on little food. They are brave men – do not force them into further suffering. Surrender now, and I will see they are fed and rested before we march for Dublin.'

He is lying, said one part of de Luzon's mind. *He is a perfidious Englishman and you cannot trust him*. But the other part – the part that craved sleep and food as a drunkard craves his wine, knew he could do little else. 'And our money and chattels?' he quibbled, hearing his own voice from a distance and amazed at his obstinacy. 'The goods we salvaged from our ship?'

'Your possessions are forfeit to the crown as spoils of war. I cannot deprive Her Majesty of what is legally hers. However, I will permit each private soldier to keep his best suit of clothes and each gentleman to retain two. That is my final offer.'

De Luzon knew he should refuse, but he felt his exhaustion pressing down like an anvil on his shoulders. He looked at his emaciated army, then bowed his head. 'Very well,' he conceded. 'I yield to your terms and trust in your honour to observe them.'

Like sleepwalkers, the starving company shuffled forward to lay down their arms. Swords, muskets and pikes were stacked in a heap before the gloating eyes of Henry Hovenden and his brother. De Luzon watched wretchedly. *See their greed*, accused his mind. *See how they count the weapons, how they calculate the reward they will get when they present them to their queen. You have sold your freedom to men who have no honour. They will not keep their promises*. His heart heard the words and knew them to be true, but he lacked the energy to worry. He swayed on his feet and imagined himself lying down and never having to rise again.

When the last weapon had been surrendered, the company moved off, bound, so the Hovendens told them, for Castle Berte – the stronghold of one, Sean O'Docherty, Lord of Inishowen. It was an agonisingly slow progress, for many of the Spaniards were too weak to walk and their companions in little state to assist them.

They had just skirted a large bog which lay between them and the castle when a commotion broke out towards the back of the column. De Luzon turned to see what was happening. An English soldier, under the guise of assisting a fallen prisoner, had pulled off the man's cloak and was searching the hems for hidden coins. The Spaniard was too weak to protest, but some of his companions had gone to his aid. As de Luzon approached, one of them shoved the soldier away.

The trooper's hand flew to his hip, a dagger flashed and one of the Spaniards staggered backwards, clutching at his chest. At once pandemonium erupted. Like wolves set loose, the troopers fell on the rest of the prisoners and began to strip them of everything they owned, tearing, ripping, dragging off boots and clothing and killing anyone who resisted.

The suddenness of the attack was as frightening as its brutality. De Luzon was bewildered. He tried feebly to push his way through the scrum. Hands seized him and threw him to the ground. They beat him, tore at him, turned and twisted him and stripped him of everything he wore. Voices screeched at each other, fighting over his possessions. He struggled helplessly. Someone grabbed him by the hair.

Then something – a fist? a musket? a knife hilt? – struck him across the side of the head and he passed out.

He came round to a sick and eerie calm: a silence, broken only by the sobs of men driven beyond endurance and the crying of the injured and the dying. The frenzy had spent itself. De Luzon shut his eyes. He never wanted to open them again. He was naked but that didn't matter; nothing mattered. All he wanted was to lie still, undisturbed, and wait for death. He felt himself sliding back into unconsciousness.

Then, not far away, a man shrieked – a wild,

gibbering sound that rose to a crescendo and ended, too suddenly, in a choking gurgle. De Luzon remembered his duty, remembered that he was a colonel in the Spanish army and that these men were in his care. He dragged himself to his feet and looked around.

The scene was like a painting of hell. Scarecrow figures staggered across a nightmare landscape, or sprawled naked on the earth, too weak or stunned to move. Some were bleeding, some were probably dead; one or two, driven over the edge into madness, crawled around on all fours, mewling like lost kittens. Around them, blood-smeared and sweating, clutching their spoils and grinning like demons out of the inferno, stood the Hovendens' troopers.

De Luzon staggered across to where Henry Hovenden stood with his brother, Richard. 'Is this how you keep your word?' he gasped. 'Is this your concept of honour? You are no better than animals. I was a fool to trust the word of an Englishman.'

Henry Hovenden's heavy features flushed with anger. His brother took a step forward. 'Have a care, what you say, Spaniard. I could have my men fillet you where you stand.'

De Luzon almost laughed. His detached mind was whispering to him with brittle clarity. 'And lose the ransom I will bring you?' he jeered. 'Your queen, who is an aging slut, with no more honour than you – who rewards you for your treachery – would not thank you for that.'

Richard Hovenden swore, and made as though to

draw his sword, but his brother laid a hand on his arm. 'I regret what has happened,' he said to de Luzon. 'It was not of my doing or by my orders. I cannot restore your belongings – my men have claimed them as trophies of war and to despoil them would be difficult and dangerous. However, the castle is only two miles distant and I promise you, you shall have clothing found for you when we reach it.'

De Luzon looked into his face and knew that he was lying. 'We cannot walk another two miles,' he said. 'Without food and rest we cannot walk another hundred yards. We are dying – all of us.'

Hovenden frowned. 'Then we shall make camp here for the night.'

'And in the morning we shall be weaker than we are today.'

'I will send to the castle,' promised Henry Hovenden, 'and see you are all fed before we move out.'

The day passed – and another night of starvation. The night was beyond imagining. Naked and defenceless, separated from his men and penned in a square formed by armed troopers, de Luzon huddled with his fellow officers through the hours of darkness, impotent against the cold and damp of the September night. None of them slept – for they knew that those who did would surely not wake again.

Morning came. There was still no sign of food, but de Luzon had not expected any. It had become obvious to him that their large number was an inconvenience to their captors – that the fewer prisoners who actually reached the castle, the better pleased the Englishmen would be. He wondered if he would make it himself. Though he had dragged his body into a sitting position he had not yet attempted to stand again and was not sure he was capable of doing so.

He looked across at the English camp. The Hovenden brothers had spent the night in comfort in their own tent. They were standing before it now, talking to a man and woman in Irish dress who had ridden over from the castle. The newcomers made an odd couple. The man was stooped and frail-looking. The woman had a hardness about her that was almost masculine. Her dark hair shone like burnished copper in the morning sun and it was she who appeared to be doing all the talking.

De Luzon wondered who they were. He sensed a new threat – though he could not imagine what it might be. He saw one of the Hovendens shake hands with the old man. Watching, de Luzon wrapped his arms around his aching chest and shivered.

The camp began to break up. The horsemen saddled up and moved out. The foot soldiers began to rouse the prisoners, prodding them to their feet and urging them to walk. As they stumbled away, de Luzon tried to count those left behind – the still forms that would never rise again. He staggered to his feet and awaited his own orders, but none came. The guards surrounding him and his fellow officers held firm and when he tried to move forward one of them shoved him back, sending him sprawling to the ground.

He lay on his back in the dirt. His all-seeing mind, hovering somewhere above him, looked down on him pitilessly. *You, know, don't you*, it said with icy logic. *You know what is going to happen now.*

'No!' De Luzon heaved himself up again. He saw his soldiers, grouped like a regiment of scarecrows on a piece of open ground, a bare two hundred yards from the camp. He saw the line of foot soldiers bearing down on them with primed muskets. He saw the cavalry on the far side of the field. 'No!' he screamed again. '*Madre de Dios*, no!' He lurched forward, but the guards seized him and held him back. And then the trumpet sounded.

six

LITTLE BY LITTLE, grim stories of the Armada's fate filtered back to Dublin. Donal's prediction had been all too accurate. On Clare Island, stronghold of the notorious Gráinne O'Malley, a hundred survivors from the *Gran Grin* had been butchered by the people of her kinsman, Dubhdarach Roe. In Galway, Tadhg na Buile O'Flaherty had made false signals to entice the *Conception* to her doom, while, on a beach near Killala, Melaghlen McCabb had waded knee-deep into the surf with his battle-axe to hack down eighty castaways from another wreck. The few survivors of these murderous onslaughts had been speedily rounded up by English troopers and executed.

The news struck bitterly at Hugh and his friends. Eoghan took it hardest – he had been so certain of a Spanish victory. He paced the floor like a caged bear, wild with rage and frustration. 'Damn them all,' he spluttered. 'The O'Malleys, the O'Flahertys, the whole misbegotten pack of them. Is it a liking they have for slavery? An army they could have had – a whole damned army – and they after hacking it to pieces on the beaches.' He whirled round on his companions. 'Have they no shame? Would The O'Donnell treat fellow Catholics so? Or my father, or yours, Donal? Would any of those men be dead and their ships after landing in the north?'

Donal shook his head. 'It's not that simple, Eoghan. Sure everyone knows the O'Malleys and the O'Flahertys are little better than pirates. But with a monster like Richard Bingham as Governor in Connaught and the whole province broken and starving – faith, what choice have they?'

'And Bingham after putting the fear of God into the local chieftains,' added Hugh. 'Threatening them with torture and death and they harbouring any castaways.'

'Ah, the butcher!' Eoghan spat on the floor. 'And who is after putting the fear of God into Bingham, eh? Well, I'll tell you for nothing, it was Fitzwilliam. The truth of it is all round the stableyards. The old queen is demanding vengeance, and himself fearing for his own neck and he leaving a single Spaniard alive on Irish soil.'

'Ducks eat frogs,' muttered Donal grimly.

'Poor sods,' said Hugh, not sure whether he meant the dead Spaniards, himself and his fellow hostages, or the western chieftains threatened and hounded into murder. It was the devil's own dilemma they were caught on, but to buy your life with the blood of a stranger and he after placing himself under your protection – dear God, what a weight that would be on a man's soul.

'You have a visitor, Master O'Donnell,' announced the Constable. 'Your father is come to Dublin and wishes to see you.'

'My father?' The news was so unexpected, Hugh felt a stab of fear. Had his mother been arrested?

'Is the Lady O'Donnell come with him?' he asked cautiously?'

'No,' said Seagar. 'He is here alone, on an errand to the Lord Deputy. He awaits you in the Lord Deputy's apartments.'

Relieved, but still mystified, Hugh followed his jailer across the courtyard to Sir William Fitzwilliam's private quarters.

He was shocked when he saw his father. In the short time since their last meeting, The O'Donnell had deteriorated even more. His iron-grey hair had grown wispy and almost white. His frame was stooped. His eyes faded and full of uncertainty. His voice, when he greeted Hugh, was almost unintelligible, and the boy realised that whatever had brought him to Dublin it was not a business that gave him any pleasure.

He felt suddenly old himself – as if he were now the adult and his father a frightened child who must be protected and comforted. He longed to fling his arms round the old man – to hold him and reassure him – but he was painfully conscious of Fitzwilliam's watching eyes. Instead he took The O'Donnell's hands and gave him a filial kiss.

'It's glad I am to see you, Father, and you coming all this way to visit me.'

The O'Donnell smiled feebly. An aide translated Hugh's words into English. Fitzwilliam smirked condescendingly at both of them. 'Your father is not here solely on your account, Master O'Donnell,' he said in Latin. 'He is come to render a service to the crown.'

'What service?' Hugh was immediately suspicious. It could not be anything good that the Englishman should be smiling so.

'He has brought me prisoners. He has delivered into my hands thirty high-ranking officers off the Spanish ship *Trinidad Valencera*, recently cast away on the shore of Inishowen.'

God Almighty! Hugh's belly lurched horribly. For a moment he actually thought he was going to vomit. He stared at his father. He tried to speak but his tongue would not form the words.

His father saw his distress. He clutched at Hugh's arm. 'For you.' He quavered, 'I did it for you, Hugh Roe. Did we not promise you – your mother and I. No stone unturned . . . whatever it might take . . .' His voice trailed off and he stared at his son with watery blue eyes. 'They promised me,' he finished lamely. 'They gave me their word of honour.'

Hugh wanted to weep. This poor old man, so confused, so trusting, so utterly unfit for this cruel game. 'They are lying to you, Father,' he said gently. 'They have no honour and no intention of keeping their word. They will hold me and they will hold your Spaniards – and laugh at you for believing otherwise.'

'That is enough,' broke in Fitzwilliam, who had been listening to the exchange with growing indignation. 'Your father did no more than his duty in bringing these men to me. There are heavy penalties for those who harbour the queen's enemies. As to your release – it is not within my own power to grant that, but I have promised to lay the matter before Her Majesty.'

'And you think she will agree to this . . . this . . . blood-bargain?'

'She may. Naturally, I cannot swear to it. No man can presume to know the queen's mind.'

'And there you have the truth of it, for doesn't it change with every passing breeze? I was after forgetting – remind me again of her fickleness.'

He spat the words in Irish and flung a mocking glance at Fitzwilliam's aide, daring him to translate them into English. When the man hesitated, he repeated them himself in Latin.

The Lord Deputy turned a delicate shade of purple. 'How dare you!' he spluttered. 'You do your cause no service by this impertinence. If you cannot keep a civil tongue in your head, I shall have you removed and given a sound whipping.'

'You would not dare.'

'You think not? You are a prisoner here, Master O'Donnell, not some honoured guest. You would do well to remember that. And as for these castaways – these

Spanish dogs for whom you show such a touching concern . . .' His eyes narrowed, as if, in his rage, he were seeking some new injury to inflict. 'Be grateful they, at least, still have their lives. Ask your father what happened to their companions.'

Hugh felt the blood drain from his face. He turned to The O'Donnell. 'Father? Please! He's lying, isn't he? Tell me he's lying.'

But the old man only mumbled incoherently. Tears trickled down his cheeks.

Fitzwilliam smiled grimly. 'They were executed, Master O'Donnell – three hundred of them – slaughtered like the wild beasts that they were, and their carcasses thrown into a bog. And thus will perish all who dare to raise swords against the English crown.'

Hugh did not speak – there were no words for what was in his heart.

Somehow he got himself through the rest of that interview and back to the safety of the gate-tower. He sat on the windowsill staring out across the rooftops – mute and shivering. Eoghan and Donal watched him in consternation. He tried to tell them what had happened, but the words still would not come. Rage, shame and misery fought in his head till he thought he would go mad. Vengeance, he thought – a life for a life, a death for a death. Fitzwilliam cannot keep me here for ever. Before I am through I will make him curse the day he set foot in this country and his old, red, hag of a queen will have nightmares about Hugh Roe O'Donnell.

On November the fourth, Fitzwilliam left Dublin on a triumphant tour of the north – 'To make certain no Spaniards remain at large in Ulster,' he told the Privy Council. 'To see what Spanish treasure he can lay his hands on,' jeered the horseboys in the stableyards. He returned on Christmas Eve, and his return brought more bad news – this time for Eoghan. The Lord Deputy had brought two prisoners back to Dublin with him, further pledges, so he said, for the rents O'Donnell kept promising but somehow always failed to deliver. One of them was Sean O'Docherty of Inishowen, the other Eoghan mac Toole O'Gallagher – Eoghan's father. Eoghan was beside himself with rage when he heard the news. He demanded to see his father and came back from the reunion in such a murderous mood that Hugh and Donal feared for his safety. 'I'll kill the swine,' he swore. 'If they hang me for it, I'll find a way to kill him.'

'And what will that achieve?' asked Donal. 'One Englishman dead, you with your head on a spike over the gate and your father maybe going the same way? Be patient, Eoghan. Your day will come. Revenge is like wine – it improves with the keeping.'

'Ha!' snorted Eoghan. 'I'll make wine out of his blood and send it to England as a New Year's gift for the old queen!' He picked up his own drink and hurled it across the room to splatter on the wall. 'And I'll give his head to the stable boys for a football,' he added darkly.

'And put up those two spindly legs of his for goal posts,' suggested Hugh. They all laughed, even Eoghan, and the battle light died slowly in his eyes. 'Ah, you have the truth of it,' he confessed. 'I'll bide my time – but I'll not be forgetting, mind.'

* * *

The following day – Christmas Day – Fitzwilliam announced that the religious celebrations would take the form of a thanksgiving for the defeat of the Armada. The whole garrison, he decreed, would attend morning service in Saint Patrick's Cathedral – and that included the hostages.

There was outrage in the gate-tower.

'Is it ourselves to be giving thanks for English victories?' demanded Eoghan. 'They'll not get me inside the doors of their church.'

'They will though,' said Donal sadly. 'They'll drag you there in chains, and you bellowing and kicking all the way, if they want to.'

'Bellowing and kicking,' said Hugh with a brittle laugh. 'Now there's a thought.'

They looked at him. 'What do you mean?' asked Donal.

'I mean you can lock a cat in a kennel, but you can't make it bark. And wouldn't the cat be making more noise than all the banshees between here and Glenmalure and it trying to get out?'

It was a moment before they understood him, but

then Eoghan chuckled. 'Isn't that the truth of it?' he agreed.

Donal shook his head. 'You're mad,' he told them. 'Do you know what they'll do to you?' But Hugh knew his heart was with them.

The hostages were marched to the cathedral in a body, under guard. It was a cavernous building – cold and unfriendly after the small, intimate churches most of them were used to. Some of the younger boys, indoctrinated from infancy on the evils of English heresy, crept through its doors like lost souls entering the jaws of hell.

Hugh did not fear the place, but as he looked about him his heart felt starved and shrivelled. Where were the candles, the tabernacle, the soft, red glow of the sanctuary lamp? Where was the incense – that pungent aroma of mystery and benediction that enfolded you the moment you entered an Irish church? Where was the joy, the reverence? He might as well have been at a council meeting in the castle chamber.

He tried to raise his mind to God, but all he could think of were the men whose deaths he was supposed to be celebrating: those three hundred starving wretches, slaughtered in cold blood to satisfy the blood-lust of the English queen; the thirty more – rotting now in some English prison, unless they had been ransomed – who had been sold like cattle in a bid to secure his own freedom.

Their pale, accusing faces seemed to float out at him from the dark corners of the cathedral. He closed his eyes and tried to will his spirit back into Tír Chonaill – to

Rathmullen, to Donegal, to his foster home at Castle Doe, and the friary chapel, so close to the waters of Sheephaven Bay, that, in moments of silence, you could hear the ripples breaking against the shore.

As his mind drifted, he began to relive the majesty of midnight mass – the church softly aglow with the light of candles, the brown-robed friars, the priest in the white vestments of Christmastide. He heard the singing – the glorious simplicity of Latin plainchant: '*Puer natus in Bethlehem, alleluia.*' The words soared heavenward, mingled inextricably with the scent and smoke of the incense, and his heart, throwing off the shackles of reality, rose to join it. '*A Boy is born in Bethlehem, alleluia, bringing joy to Jerusalem, alleluia. With one accord let us adore . . .*'

The shuffling of feet dragged him back to earth. He opened his eyes. The Dublin gentry, resplendent in their foreign attire, had risen for the singing of the processional hymn. Their alien music shattered his daydream. Something snapped inside him. He scrambled to his feet. 'Heretics,' he roared. 'Damned English heretics!'

Pandemonium erupted. As men-at-arms rushed over to silence him, the other hostages took up the chorus. They yelled, they whistled, they hooted and stamped their feet. They fought and struggled with their guards, till eventually they were all dragged from the cathedral and hustled, battered but triumphant, back to their prison.

Hugh, Eoghan and Donal were thrown into a cell beneath the gate-tower. 'And there you can stay till after

Epiphany,' Stephen Seagar told them furiously. 'And we'll see how you enjoy a diet of bread and water for twelve days. If you behave like animals, then, by God, that's how you'll be treated.'

He went out, slamming the door behind him. The boys looked at one another. Eoghan began to laugh. 'They'll not be taking us back there in a hurry.'

Donal rubbed his jaw. 'Isn't that the truth of it. A painful victory, but worth every bruise, I'm thinking.'

Hugh sat on the floor and leaned his back against the wall. The anger had drained from him and he felt very tired. Had it been a victory? It was hard to tell. All he knew was it had left him more miserable than ever. The dead Spanish faces still haunted him, and images of home tormented him with homesickness. The eagle high above the Fanad peninsula, snow falling softly over Bearnas Mór, the dark, bubbling waters of Lough Swilly – he yearned for them with an ache that was almost physical. Would he ever feel grass beneath his feet again, or watch trees bending in the wind, or dip cupped hands into a running stream?

He closed his eyes and, tipping his head back against the wall, began to sing – softly at first but with a growing resonance. His voice drifted out through the grille high in the wall and floated across the courtyard. Churchgoers, returning to the castle from their disrupted service, paused for a moment to listen, before hurrying in to their Christmas dinners.

'Veni, veni, Emmanuel
Captivum solve Israel,
Qui gemit in exilio,
Privatus Dei Filio.
Gaude, gaude, Emmanuel
Nascetur pro te Israel.'

Oh, come, oh, come, Emmanuel,
And ransom captive Israel,
That waits in lowly exile here,
Until the son of man appears.
Rejoice, rejoice, Emmanuel
Shall come to thee, oh Israel.

seven

IT WAS A lonely Christmas, but no worse perhaps than any other spent in captivity – and at least they had one another for company. After twelve cold and hungry nights, Donal and Eoghan were finally released back to their room in the gate-tower. Hugh, however, found himself hauled off for another interview with the Lord Deputy. 'And right well he knows where to look for the ringleader in this business,' said Seagar. 'You have been nothing but trouble since the day you arrived here. You'll be lucky if you escape with a beating. If I were the Lord Deputy, I'd throw you into one of the underground dungeons in the "grate" and leave you there.'

'And bring the northern clans down about your ears like a hornets' nest,' jeered Hugh. 'You are a fool, Seagar. Fitzwilliam dare not punish me. My father and Hugh mac Ferdoragh learn of everything that passes here. They would make a noose out of his own guts for the man who laid a hand on me.'

It was a comforting boast, but not very truthful – and

Hugh knew it. Despite his bravado he had a battle to hide his fear when he was ushered into the Lord Deputy's presence.

But Fitzwilliam, it seemed, was in a generous mood. He greeted the boy with a smile and beckoned him forward, waving Seagar back to wait by the door. The Lord Deputy was seated behind a huge oak table, and he had someone with him – Miler Magrath, the Archbishop of Cashel. Magrath had been a Catholic before he had seen the light – and been well rewarded for his conversion. The Archbishop smiled unctuously at his young countryman. Hugh scowled.

'Be seated, Master O'Donnell,' invited the Lord Deputy. Hugh looked at the low stool, deliberately placed, he suspected, so the two men would be able to look down at him. He debated whether to refuse it, decided it was not worth the effort and sat.

The Lord Deputy leaned back in his chair and studied him, much as one might appraise a puppy presented for inspection. Hugh stared back. If Perrot had resembled a bull, then Fitzwilliam, he decided, was a fox – nervous and fussy, with sharp eyes and a shrewd, narrow face. He remembered what Hugh mac Ferdoragh had said about the man – that he was not wealthy, and might therefore be bribable. Was it true? Did those eyes reflect greed or only meanness?

Finally, as Fitzwilliam continued to stare at him, his curiosity turned to irritation. 'Is there something amiss with my face, my Lord Deputy?' he demanded. 'Have I leprosy perhaps – or the first signs of smallpox?'

Fitzwilliam only smiled. 'On the contrary, Master O'Donnell, it is a very pleasing face – well-favoured and intelligent. I can see why your father sets such store by you.'

'Then why do you keep me a prisoner in your castle when I should be at his side?'

'Come now, Master Hugh, we have been through this before. It was not I who sent that ship to Lough Swilly.'

'But it is you who keeps me here. Does that make you less guilty?'

'Enough.' Fitzwilliam was starting to lose patience. 'You are here by Her Majesty's command. You know as well as I do, the custom of hostage is a perfectly legal one. Does not your own father take pledges from his client chieftains?'

'Not by abduction. I am not a pledge, I am a prisoner.'

'You draw a fine distinction.'

'I do not. Hugh mac Ferdoragh gave pledges last time he came to Dublin. Were they locked up in the gate-tower and threatened with chains if they caused trouble? No. They were lodged in the city with only their word to hold them.'

Fitzwilliam pretended to consider this statement. 'And would you give your word if it were asked of you?'

'Would you take it if I gave it?'

The Lord Deputy did not answer and Hugh knew he had won that round. Archbishop Magrath broke the silence. Folding his hands over his Book of Common

Prayer, which lay on the table in front of him, he said, speaking in Latin for Fitzwilliam's benefit, 'I was grieved, Master O'Donnell, to learn that you and your friends have refused spiritual consolation.'

It took Hugh a moment to realise what he was talking about. It was hardly the way he would have described the Christmas fiasco. 'We have not refused it, Master Magrath,' he said coldly. 'We have been denied it.'

'Indeed? That is not how it was told to me, but if it be true, it can soon be remedied.'

'You mean we may have a priest to say mass for us?'

'Indeed, I do not. I mean there are many good churchmen in Dublin who would be pleased to instruct you in the true faith.'

'We do not want your heresies. We want our mass.'

'You are being impertinent, boy,' broke in Fitzwilliam. 'And it is your popish mass that is heresy – seditious blasphemy gabbled in an incomprehensible tongue.'

'I do not find Latin incomprehensible.'

'Perhaps not – you have been taught to speak it. But what of your humbler clansmen? Of what benefit to them are scriptures read in a language they cannot understand?'

Hugh stared at him. Was the man really as stupid as he appeared? He stretched a hand across the table. 'Show me the book you use for your services,' he demanded of Magrath. The Archbishop handed him his prayer book. Hugh opened it. He turned a couple of pages, then held it up triumphantly to Fitzwilliam. 'You see,' he said. 'It is all in English.'

The Lord Deputy looked perplexed. 'Well, of course it is. What did you expect?'

Mother of God! This was worse than teaching the catechism to a six-year-old. 'My clansmen, those humble folk who do not speak Latin, they do not speak English either – and no more do I.'

Light dawned in Fitzwilliam's eyes. He smiled reassuringly. 'You need not be ashamed of your ignorance. What opportunity have you had to learn better – or your countrymen – living the remote and savage lives you do? But all that is going to change. It is Her Majesty's greatest wish that you should be taught and civilised.'

'Civilised! And . . . and it is her belief that to speak English is to be civilised?'

'Of course. That is the start. With the language come the customs and the manners. Once you understand our ways you will see how much better they are. We will teach you to build proper houses, and towns and –'

I am going to scream, thought Hugh. It is like beating your head against a wall. 'We do not want your towns,' he said patiently, 'nor your houses nor your customs nor your language. We are . . .' He took a deep breath. 'WE – ARE – NOT – ENGLISH.'

Fitzwilliam's understanding smile expanded across his whole face. 'Of course you are not, but that is not your fault. We shall just have to do the best we can.'

Hugh stood up. Blood sang in his brain. He watched his own hands lay the book down on the table. He saw them open it and tear out half a dozen pages. He watched his fingers rip the paper into tiny shreds and fling them like a snow-storm into Fitzwilliam's face. 'To hell with your English prayer book,' he exploded. 'And to hell with everything else English, too.' And he turned to storm out of the room.

Seagar, who had been waiting patiently by the door, grabbed him by the collar and one wrist, jerked his arm up behind his back and twisted him round to face the Lord Deputy. Fitzwilliam stared at him in amazement. Then – 'Put him back in his cell and let him cool his heels there for a few more days,' he ordered the Constable. 'Let us hope it restores him to his senses.'

Seagar marched the boy out. Fitzwilliam sat in bewilderment staring at the place where Hugh had stood. What on earth had he said or done to provoke such an extraordinary outburst? He wondered whether to ask the Archbishop, but decided against it. Magrath was Irish himself and, despite his loyalty, not quite to be relied on. Fitzwilliam recalled his predecessor's assessment of young O'Donnell. Well, Sir John, he thought grimly, it seems there is, after all, one point on which we both agree. You can do your best for these barbarians – dress them decently, educate them, give them a veneer of civilisation – but then, just when you think you have them eating out of your hand, some unpredictable little incident sets them off again and they revert straight back to their old savagery.

He sighed, thinking of the lucrative offers he had been made in Donegal and Dungannon – the veiled suggestions, the whispered promises. He had been very tempted, but the risk was simply too great. His duty was clear.

Taking his leave of Archbishop Magrath, Fitzwilliam returned to his private chamber and the letter he had begun to write earlier in the day – a report to Her Majesty's Privy Council. Dipping his pen into the ink, he added another careful sentence. *And further would I warn you*, he wrote, *of the dangers that might grow unto this miserable realm, by letting loose the reins unto so harebrained and ingracious an imp as O'Donnell's son.*

The 'harebrained imp' spent another ten days in the cell beneath the gate-tower, reflecting on his ungracious behaviour. He could have avoided it. 'The Lord Deputy is prepared to be magnanimous,' announced Seagar after the first day. 'An apology is all it will take to unlock your door.' But Hugh could not bring himself to give one. What had he to apologise for? Fitzwilliam was the one at fault, with his absurd notions about civilisation.

Did the Lord Deputy really imagine his English manners, his language or his ridiculous clothes were things any sane Irishman would ever covet? Did all Saxons hold the same belief? If so, then their conceit was only matched by their stupidity.

Hugh told Seagar what the Lord Deputy could do with his magnanimity, gritted his teeth and put up with his solitary confinement.

Eventually, however, Fitzwilliam decided the boy had been punished enough. He was let out and Seagar – with many threats of what would happen if he misbehaved again – escorted him back to the gate-tower. It was a great relief. Despite his bravado, Hugh had been growing heartily sick of his own company. He was also spoiling for exercise. Even the confines of the castle yards would seem like freedom after three weeks in a cell. And he could hardly wait to see Eoghan and Donal again and tell them about his confrontation with Fitzwilliam and Magrath. Eoghan, especially, would enjoy the story.

He ran up the gate-tower stairs, two at a time, leaving Seagar to plod after him, but when he flung open the door of their room it was neither of his friends who greeted him. Instead, he was met by two other hostages, Hugh O'Toole and Art Kavanagh. He knew both these young men. Hugh was the brother of Felim O'Toole of Castlekevin and brother-in-law to the notorious Fiach mac Hugh. He had been given as a pledge for Fiach's good behaviour when the Glenmalure chieftain attended Perrot's farewell celebrations. And, in typical fashion, the English had *forgotten* to release him. Art Kavanagh had come quite recently, as pledge for one of his kinsmen. He was older than most of the others and already had a reputation as a swordsman.

Hugh stared at them. 'Where's Eoghan? Where's Donal?' he demanded. He swung round accusingly on Seagar. 'What are you after doing with them?'

Seagar smirked. 'They've abandoned you,' he jeered.

'They must have grown tired of your company.'

Hugh didn't understand. Alarming possibilities rioted through his mind, but Art Kavanagh reassured him. 'They escaped,' he explained with a broad grin.

'Escaped! How? When?'

'Two days ago. Didn't someone *accidentally* leave a door unlocked and they through it and off like the wild hunt.'

'But . . .' Hugh's mind reeled. People didn't escape that easily from Dublin Castle. There was more to this than Art was letting on. Money must have changed hands somewhere along the line and he had a pretty good idea who had been the giver – and the taker. 'I want to see Eoghan mac Toole O'Gallagher,' he demanded.

'Do you now,' said the Constable. 'And who are you to be making demands?'

Nevertheless, the request must have been passed on to the Lord Deputy, for a couple of days later Hugh was permitted to visit Eoghan's father. It was a strained meeting. Hugh felt betrayed. Eoghan mac Toole had been his foster father for several years – had treated him as his own son. How could he now have abandoned him so shamefully? 'It was you, wasn't it?' he demanded as soon as they were alone together. 'You bribed the Lord Deputy and he to turn his back while Eoghan and Donal escaped.'

'I did,' admitted O'Gallagher.

'And you knowing all the time that I was locked away and not able to go with them. Was your purse not big enough for three of us?'

The older man shook his head. 'Ah, Hugh, do you think we did not try? I, your mother, Hugh mac Ferdoragh – a king's ransom we offered for you, but for all his greed, Fitzwilliam is no fool and you are the most valuable hostage he holds. The English queen is as cruel and grasping as the Morrigu – and as little forgiving of those who cross her. What use could your man make of all our gold, and he with no head on his shoulders?'

Hugh said nothing. He felt cold and empty. The claws of the old red queen clutched at his entrails like meat hooks. She could keep him here forever – till he grew old and feeble and his heart broke and he died. He wanted to be happy for Eoghan and Donal, but the sense of abandonment was almost unbearable. It was as though someone had kicked his feet from under him and left him drowning in a bog.

His foster father put strong hands on his shoulders. 'Have faith, son. We are not after deserting you. Hugh mac Ferdoragh has powerful friends. If he can't buy your freedom, he'll find a way to steal it – and mine too, eventually, please God.'

His voice faltered over those last few words. Hugh felt a prick of conscience. In the heat of his own disappointment, he had forgotten that O'Gallagher, also, was a captive. 'I'm sorry,' he said. 'I had no right to say the things I did.'

He crossed to the window and looked out at the familiar skyline. The rooftops were grey and wet, but the clouds were thinning and there was a rainbow in the western sky. He gazed at it. It arched across the heavens – a bright promise, stretching from Dublin to Donegal. And somewhere beneath it, Eoghan and Donal were making their way north to freedom. Hope crept back into his heart. 'God guide the journey,' he whispered, and he smiled at O'Gallagher.

eight

IN A PUBLIC show of precaution against further accidents, Fitzwilliam ordered that, from now on, the more valuable hostages were to be moved to stronger prisons each night though they still spent their days in the gate-tower. On the first evening of his so-called freedom, Hugh found himself back in his old cell beneath the gate-tower.

It was difficult to keep cheerful, alone in the darkness after the door had closed. But he knew things could have been a lot worse. At least this cell was dry and reasonably clean. He had unpleasant dreams sometimes about those other prisons he had never seen – the terrible dungeons in what they called the 'grate'.

The first three nights passed without incident, but on the fourth he was jolted from sleep by footsteps clattering down the stairwell. He sat up in alarm. In the blackness he heard a key rattle in his lock, the door swing open, English voices growling incomprehensibly. And something – someone? – was thrust into the cell. Then the door slammed and was locked again.

He peered into the darkness. 'Who is it? Who's there?'

'Hugh?' croaked a weary voice. 'Hugh, is it yourself?'

'Donal!' He scrambled across the floor and flung his arms round his friend. Donal shivered. His clothes were wet. His hands and cheeks felt as cold as marble. He sagged in Hugh's arms as though his legs were too weak to support him.

Hugh dragged him over to the sleeping place, packed the straw round him and spread his own cloak over the top. He touched Donal's face. It was like touching a corpse. 'Mother of God,' he breathed. 'What are they after doing to you?'

Donal tried to speak, but his teeth were chattering too hard. Hugh laid a hand over his mouth. 'Leave it rest,' he said. 'Get some sleep. You can tell me in the morning.'

Donal muttered incoherently. His eyes closed. After a while his muscles relaxed and his breathing became deeper and more regular. Hugh's mind was in turmoil. What had gone wrong? Where was Eoghan? Had he been recaptured too? Hugh sat down beside Donal, intending to watch over him while he slept, but his own eyes were heavy and he was bitterly cold without his cloak. After shivering for what seemed ages, he finally burrowed into the straw beside his friend and fell asleep.

He was wakened by the footsteps of the guard, coming to escort them back to the gate-tower. Sitting up, he pushed straw out of his face and looked over at Donal. The older boy was asleep. It was still too dark to see his face properly but his cheek was warm to the touch and he appeared peaceful and relaxed.

The door opened and the light of a lantern flooded the cell. Donal stirred. His eyes opened. He raised himself on one elbow and stared around him as if trying to remember where he was. 'Ah damn it!' he swore, and sank back into the straw again.

'Welcome back,' said Hugh dryly. 'Will I order the stewards to bring food for you?'

Donal sneezed.

It was a lame horse had brought him undone. 'And we after reaching Glenmalure with no trouble at all,' he said sadly when they were reunited with Art Kavanagh and Hugh O'Toole in the tower-top room. 'And Fiach mac Hugh feasting us like heroes and giving us two fine mounts to carry us north. But didn't mine go lame on me, and we no more than a cock's crow from Drogheda? I had to walk her and they seized me at the bridge.'

'And Eoghan? asked Hugh O'Toole.

'Eoghan was still mounted, so I shouted at him to run – no sense us both getting caught. He went through that town as fast as a dose of pox through an English castle and, the last I saw of him, he was still heading north as though the hounds of hell were at his heels.' He grinned. 'And so they were, in a manner of speaking.'

They all laughed. 'A good man it would take to outride Eoghan O'Gallagher, and him on a good horse and the scent of home in his nostrils,' observed Art Kavanagh. 'And they brought you straight back to Dublin?'

'They did – and with the weather that was in it, and the soldiers cursing and cuffing me all the way, wasn't I glad enough to see the place.' He looked around the room and grinned defiantly, but Hugh was not deceived. To have tasted freedom, and then had it snatched away like that – he could imagine how his friend was feeling.

❋ ❋ ❋

Luckily Donal took nothing more than a heavy cold from his adventures. Within a few days he was fully recovered and life slipped back into its old routine. Boredom was the chief enemy. They had their liberty in the yards during the daytime but there was little to do except talk, play *ficheall* and *brandubh* with the other hostages and read books – Latin texts provided by their captors or the few Irish ones smuggled in by visitors.

At least they were still allowed visitors. Hugh O'Toole's brother, Felim, came frequently and several of Hugh mac Ferdoragh's friends. They brought gifts and news from home – though the news was a mixed blessing. Conditions in Tír Chonaill were becoming increasingly grim.

'The O'Donnell is failing fast,' Felim told Hugh sadly, 'and the Lord Deputy takes advantage of it. Fitzwilliam still has his pack of dogs in Donegal Friary. And your half-brother, Donnell, is rallying his supporters and preparing to depose your father.'

'And my mother?' asked Hugh anxiously.

Felim chuckled. 'The Iníon Dubh is gone to Scotland to hire gallowglasses. And didn't she burn down Donegal Castle before she went, to keep it out of the hands of her stepson and his English allies?'

And she the wise one. But the images conjured up by Felim's words were almost unbearable. Donegal Castle a charred ruin; drunken soldiers still carousing in the cloisters of the friary – Hugh's mind revolted against these horrors and the frustration of his own helplessness nearly drove him insane. 'I should be there,' he raged at Donal, in the confines of their night-time prison. 'I should be there with my mother – I should be at her side with your father and The MacSweeney Doe – not rotting in this stinking hole.' And he pounded his fists on the wall.

'We should both be there,' said Donal patiently. 'But we're not, and ranting and raving will change nothing. The best thing you can do, and you wanting to help them, is to pray for them.'

So he tried, but it was useless. Even his faith seemed prisoner in this place. His thoughts went round like rats in a barrel and finally came back to fester in his head. He found himself railing at God – who had once sent an angel to break Saint Peter out of prison – for not doing more on his behalf.

The Iníon Dubh was back in Ireland before the end of summer, and in September Felim at last brought a piece of good news. Donnell O'Donnell was dead. 'A battle there was,' declared Felim. 'A great uproar of a fight near Doire Leathain between his army and the gallowglasses of the Iníon Dubh. All day long they say it raged, up and down and to and fro, as fierce as the legendary cattle raid of Cooley. And your half-brother getting his death at the hands of The MacSweeney Doe's men.'

Donnell dead! Hugh's first instinct was to cheer. Later, though, as his glee abated, it left behind something horribly like guilt. He did not grieve for Donnell. He had hardly known the man – for all that they were half-brothers – and Donnell had certainly never wished him well. But Hugh knew the real reason for his death. Donnell had stood between Hugh and the chieftaincy and the Iníon Dubh had dispatched him without remorse.

He was the second such pretender she had removed. And from a bog on Inishowen three hundred Spanish souls still cried out for vengeance. The blood-debt was rising all the time, and he trapped behind the walls of Dublin Castle – a playing piece, shuffled round a political *ficheall* board and as powerless as a carved token to influence the playing of the game.

Another Christmas passed – the third of his captivity, another Easter, another summer. Hugh mac Ferdoragh continued to petition and intrigue on Hugh's behalf, but his pleas fell on deaf ears. Fitzwilliam seemed to find them amusing. 'He wastes his efforts,' he informed Hugh, during one of their interviews. 'No man in the castle dare take his money, and the Privy Council are unshakable in their resolve to keep you here. But they encourage him to beg. It keeps him obedient and submissive.'

Hugh said nothing.

'He claims you are his son-in-law.'

'Does he?'

'Well?'

'Well, what?'

'Is it true?'

Hugh thought carefully. 'Would Hugh mac Ferdoragh tell a lie?'

Fitzwilliam's lip curled. 'The Earl of Tyrone is the most consummate liar I have ever met. That is why I am asking you.'

'And am I not also a liar – an Irish savage, suckled on mendacity at my mother's breast? Whether I say yes or no – how will you believe me?'

The Lord Deputy scowled. 'How indeed,' he said disgustedly. 'You are all the same. God knows we have tried to teach you better, but you are as untrustworthy as a pack of wolves.' He waved a hand at Seagar. 'Take him out.'

Hugh went back to the gate-tower in silence. He turned the words over in his mind. He thought of the broken English promises, the gruesome trophies above the castle gate. He knew who the real wolves were.

● ● ●

Winter came early that year. As the wind swung round to the north and the rain turned to sleet that flailed the castle walls and melted into dirty puddles in the yards, Hugh's spirits reached their lowest ebb. He had been a prisoner now for three years and he was losing hope. He slept badly; he quarrelled with Art Kavanagh and Hugh O'Toole; he sat for hours at the gate-tower window, staring out across the Liffey, trying to pretend the distant hills were the mountains of Tír Chonaill. I shall go mad, he thought, and I not getting out of this place soon.

A few weeks before Christmas they had a new visitor – an Englishman.

'Richard Weston,' the young man introduced himself, as he was shown into their room, 'a friend of Hugh mac Ferdoragh's, come at his bidding to see how you are faring.'

He had an easy manner on him and fluent Irish. The others greeted him cordially, but Hugh didn't trust him. Nicholas Barnes, the skipper of the *Matthew*, had spoken Irish too – and been just as charming.

'And what dealings has Hugh mac Ferdoragh with a lackey of the English queen?' Hugh demanded.

The young man smiled, unfazed by the hostility. 'He sends letters to you.' He reached inside his doublet – the most garish and ridiculously padded garment Hugh had ever seen – and pulled out several folded parchments.

Hugh took them, ungraciously. He turned them over in his hand and saw that the seals had all been broken. 'Letters is it?' he said bitterly. 'And the Lord Deputy after reading every one of them.'

Weston shrugged.

'Ah, Hugh,' remonstrated Donal, 'where is your gratitude? The man is good enough to bring letters for us. Is it his place to be hiding them from the Lord Deputy?'

'It is not then,' said Hugh contemptuously, 'for they might be after searching him, and tearing that fancy coat he's wearing.'

The young man grinned broadly. 'Isn't that the truth of it,' he said. 'And maybe finding what I have underneath it.' He opened the door and looked quickly up and down the stairwell. Then he turned to Art Kavanagh. 'You look like a man with a good, hefty shoulder. Put it against the door for a moment.'

Art looked baffled, but good-naturedly he leaned his back against the door. Dick Weston removed his doublet and then, to Hugh's amazement, began to peel off his undershirts.

At last he stood naked to the waist. They stared at him. '*Chreesta*,' spluttered Donal. He began to laugh and Hugh felt the spiteful words he'd uttered twist in his heart to shame him. No wonder Weston's doublet had looked so bulky. Underneath it, wrapped around his chest, was a length of thin, silken rope.

'A present from Hugh mac Ferdoragh,' grinned Weston, as the boys hastily unwound the rope and buried it in their clothes-chest. 'It's as much as I dared to bring at the one time, but you'll be having other visitors. By Twelfth Night . . .' he made an expansive gesture with his hands.

Donal shook his head wonderingly. 'It's a brave man you are, Dick Weston.'

Art and Hugh O'Toole crowded round to add their own thanks. Hugh Roe could only hang his head. 'I'm sorry,' he mumbled. 'I spoke out of my own dirty temper. What can I say?'

'Nothing,' said Weston. 'Just keep that door shut till I have myself dressed again.' He laughed at Hugh's woebegone face. 'Ah, don't be slighting yourself, Hugh Roe. Wouldn't I be after saying the same things and I shut up in this place as long as you?'

It was generous of him, but Hugh still felt ashamed. Won't I learn to bite my tongue in future, he promised himself, before taking my frustrations out on others.

Over a flagon of wine – a present left over from Felim O'Toole's last visit – the young men discussed plans. 'It will have to be done after dark,' said Hugh O'Toole, 'and no one to see us climbing down the wall. What time do they close the city gates?'

'About an hour after sunset,' Weston told him.

They looked at one another. 'And the guards coming to take us to our night-time cells at about the same time,' said Donal. 'We'll not have much of a start on them.'

'Could we not barricade our door?' suggested Art.

Hugh shook his head. 'They'd guess we were making an escape. But if there was some way to bolt the castle door and we safely on the outside . . .'

Dick Weston frowned for a moment. Then he started to laugh. 'Ah, you're as smart as a pet fox, Hugh Roe

O'Donnell. Sure and isn't there a great iron ring on the outside of the castle door, with a chain on it for a man to pull the door shut behind him and he after going out? A bar of wood driven through that ring and across the door jamb would hold it against an army and they trapped inside.'

'And a rope let down from this window will drop us on the bridge right in front of it,' added Hugh. 'But where will we get a stave? We can't carry one down the wall.'

'I'll have a man waiting for you, and he to bring one,' Weston promised him.

'But how will he know when we are ready to make our break?' asked Donal. 'We won't know ourselves until the time is right.'

'He'll be watching. Once you have enough rope, I'll have someone near the bridge each evening until you are safe away.'

The boys looked at each other speechless with excitement. 'Ah, you're the man in the gap and no mistake,' declared Donal at last, 'the hero of the hour. But it's a great risk you are taking. What do you get out of it?'

Dick Weston grinned. 'Hugh mac Ferdoragh is generous to his friends,' he said slyly. 'And, forbye, it's little liking I have for the Lord Deputy.'

It was the best Christmas in Hugh's three years of captivity. The days passed in a whirl of suppressed excitement and he had to struggle at times to hide his elation from his captors. Dick Weston came twice more to see them. Fergus O'Farrell, of Longford, also honoured them with a visit and two of his sons came with Christmas gifts. By the end of the holiday it seemed to Hugh that every man in or around Dublin whom he had ever called a friend had climbed the gate-tower stairs to wish him the blessings of the season. Each visitor brought greetings from Hugh mac Ferdoragh and each left a little thinner than he had come in. By Twelfth Night the knotted rope had grown almost too long for concealment.

It was Weston himself who smuggled in the final length. 'You'll be right now,' he told them. 'Even allowing for the knots, it should be long enough to put you onto the bridge. Pick your time carefully, and don't try to go north – they'll be watching every road from here to Dundalk. Get up into the mountains and make for Glenmalure. Fiach mac Hugh will see you safe.' He offered a hand to each of them. 'God speed the journey,' he said and left as jauntily as he had come, his whistle floating back to them as he went down the stairs.

In the silence that followed, Hugh's heart turned cartwheels. Could this really be happening? Dare he allow himself to hope? Was it possible that after three years he was finally going to be free? He looked at the others and saw they were thinking the same things. He tried to remember what freedom felt like. Visions of Tír Chonaill crowded his mind – cuckoos calling in the woods of Bearnas Mór, the smell of the gorse round Kilmacrennan, Lough Swilly asleep in the evening sunshine.

Lough Swilly. He recalled it as he had last seen it – the fishing curraghs drawn up on its banks, the eagle above the peninsular, the forests of Inishowen sweeping down to its shoreline-. . . the dark waters slapping round the hull of the *Matthew*. How much would it have changed in three years? How much had *he* changed? He had been a child that day; but his childhood was long gone – buried in a bog on Inishowen with three hundred murdered Spaniards – and all the faery magic of the Sidhe would never bring it back again. He squared his shoulders. If he could not rewrite the past, at least the future was still his. He had a life to live – and debts of honour to repay.

nine

NOW THEY HAD the means of escape, it was tempting to take their chance that very night, but Donal urged caution. So many things had to be right. They needed a cloudy or moonless night. The streets round the castle had to be empty. There must be time enough for them to get safely out of the city before they were missed. 'We'll only have the one chance,' Donal warned them. 'We mustn't waste it.'

So they watched and waited, forcing themselves to be patient, and, at last, a full week after Twelfth Night, everything finally fell into place. It had been a bleak day and darkness came early – an evening of thick cloud and drifting snowflakes.

'As black as an Englishman's guts,' declared Art Kavanagh as he peered out into the gloom from his perch on the windowsill. 'You'd hardly see your hand before your face with the weather that's in it, and everyone away home early to their firesides. The streets are deserted.'

'And the castle gate?' asked Donal, trying to look over his shoulder.

Art looked down. 'They're closing it now. The sentries are all in off the bridge.' He slid from the windowsill and looked from one to the other of his companions. 'We'll not have a better chance, I'm telling you.'

'Then what are we waiting for?' said Hugh. He flung open the chest and pulled out the rope.

The others dragged the heavy oak table over to the window and Art secured the rope to one of the table legs. Hugh O'Toole jammed a chair under the handle of the door to wedge it shut. 'In case anyone tries to come in and we only halfway down the wall,' he said.

Art tossed the rope out the window. 'We'll go in order of age,' he whispered. 'You first, Hugh Roe, then Donal, and Hugh and I to follow.'

Hugh scrambled onto the windowsill. He looked down at the bridge. He had never appreciated before what a long way down it was. The thin, silken rope felt absurdly flimsy between his hands. For a moment his heart failed him; then he thought again of Lough Swilly, of the English soldiers in Donegal Friary, of a wrecked ship and three hundred men who should still have been alive. He wriggled backwards through the window, wrapped his legs around the rope and began the long descent.

It took an eternity – his arms ached, his knees and elbows scraped against the wall, the thin rope cut his hands – but suddenly his feet touched stone and he was standing on the parapet of the bridge. He dropped to the ground and looked up at the tower. It loomed over him, blacker than the darkness of the night. *Dhia*! he thought, did I really escape from there? As he watched, he saw a dark figure squeeze through the window and begin its descent – Donal. Hugh fought down the urge to shout in triumph. They were going to make it – all of them – he knew they were.

But he must get off the bridge, he was too conspicuous. Feeling his way cautiously, he edged along the wall to the safety of the street. There was not a sound from the castle. It was almost too easy. His mind danced – running ahead of him to Glenmalure, boasting to Fiach mac Hugh of their high deeds and daring escapades – then, just as he stepped off the bridge a shadow loomed out of the darkness at his side. Before he could utter a sound, a strong arm flung him to the ground and a hand was clapped across his mouth.

He struggled. A face bent over him and a voice whispered in his ear: 'Hold your noise. I'm a friend. Cormac O'Hanley, kerne to Fergus O'Farrell of Longford.'

O'Farrell's man! Hugh could have wept with relief. This must be the guide Dick Weston had promised. He let himself go limp and after a moment the hand was taken from his mouth. 'Hugh Roe O'Donnell,' he whispered, feeling extremely foolish.

'My sorrow, Hugh Roe. It's no wish I had to scare you, but I dared not let you call out.'

'And you the wise one.' Hugh scrambled to his feet.

'I'll warn the others as they come off the bridge.'

Before long, all four of them were crouched safely with their guide behind the wall of the moat. 'We must waste no time,' whispered Cormac. 'They'll be shutting the city gate soon.' He reached inside his cloak. 'Here, I have swords for you. And this also – O'Farrell said you would be needing it.'

He put something into Hugh's hand – something long and smooth and wooden. Hugh did not need to ask what it was. Weston had remembered.

With the stave in his hand and a sword thrust through his belt he crept back across the bridge. His heart thumped as he approached the great door. There was the ring just as Weston had described it. It would take only a moment to secure it. But . . . Hugh's ears strained in the darkness. Was that a shout? Had they been missed already? At any moment the door might fly open and spew men onto the bridge with pikes and guns – and himself alone here.

Gritting his teeth, Hugh lifted the stave and drove it through the iron ring. It fitted as smoothly as a hand going into a glove – not a hair's breadth to spare. Hugh's confidence soared. Swiftly he eased the pole through till a good half of its length was wedged across the door jamb, then, hugging his triumph, he ran back to his companions.

'Did you wedge it good and tight, now?' whispered Cormac.

'As tight as the truth in a Saxon's mouth. They'll not shake it loose and they trying till doomsday.'

'Good man. Then let's go.'

With Cormac leading the way and Art Kavanagh covering their rear, the young men set off through the silent streets. Hugh had to fight back the urge to keep glancing over his shoulder. How long before their flight was discovered and the shouts of the garrison brought someone from outside to unbar the door? And what if the city gate was closed? Or they were challenged?

Hugh slipped a hand inside his cloak to touch his sword and tried to pretend confidence.

By the wall of Saint Werburgh's church, Cormac halted his little band. 'We'll not all attempt the gate together,' he said. 'Hugh Roe and I will go first, and you following us after a few moments.' He looked at Hugh. 'Are you ready?'

Hugh nodded. He felt anything but ready, but there was no use putting it off. By the dim glow of the street lanterns, he looked towards the gate and the little bridge over the Poddle. The wall here was an extension of the castle wall. To the east, rising above the church, he could see the massive bulk of the Bermingham Tower. He imagined eyes watching him from its windows – muskets trained on his back as he crossed the bridge. 'Patrick defend me,' he prayed, and, gritting his teeth, marched after Cormac.

As if in answer to his prayer, a sudden flurry of snow swirled round his ears. By the time he reached the gate he could barely see Cormac, three strides in front of him. They passed unchallenged. The sentries, huddled in their cloaks, hardly spared them a glance and the few people they passed had their heads down and were too intent on hurrying home to notice two nondescript figures going the other way. Hugh chuckled silently as he offered up his thanks. However much the English might try to forbid the wearing of it, an Irish mantle was a very inconspicuous garment on a winter's night – even in Dublin.

Once clear of the bridge, Cormac led them at a purposeful but unhurried pace through the outlying suburbs. The streets were empty, but they walked in wary silence. Hugh's body was still tensed against a half-expected challenge. He kept his right hand on the hilt of his sword and guessed that Art was doing the same.

And then, quite suddenly, it seemed, the last of the houses was behind them and they were in open countryside. They walked on for a while, then Cormac stopped and pointed into the distance. 'Look,' he said. 'The Wicklow Mountains.'

Hugh followed his gaze. The snow clouds that had covered their escape were starting to break up. He could see trees and grassland – the Irish countryside stretching away before him to the black slopes of Slieve Roe. He sucked in a lungful of cold, sweet air.

He wanted to shout and dance, to seize fistfuls of turf and fling them into the wind. He was free! No more locked doors or grey stone walls – he could run as far as he wished in any direction, with nothing to restrain him.

❋ ❋ ❋

By morning the euphoria had faded. They had walked all night, climbing higher and higher into the mountains, and Hugh was exhausted. Three years in prison had been hardly the best training for such an expedition. Worse still, his shoes were coming apart – they were thin, English shoes, never intended for outdoor use – and his feet were bruised and blistered. He plodded grimly after the others, each step an increasing agony, praying for sleep and daylight and the safety of Ballinacor – Fiach mac Hugh's stronghold in Glenmalure.

Towards dawn, Cormac halted the party for a brief rest in the shelter of a wood. The clouds had returned – this time bringing rain – and everyone was cold, wet and hungry.

'How much further?' grumbled Art, flopping onto the wet grass.

'Only an hour or so,' said Cormac. 'We are near Glendalough. You would see the tower from here – and the clouds not hiding it.'

'An hour, is it? *Dhia*, but I'll be glad to see Ballinacor.' Donal also dropped to the ground and began to massage his aching calf muscles. 'I've a hunger on me like a friar on Good Friday, and I'll say this for Fiach mac Hugh – he keeps a grand table.'

'Ah, he does that,' agreed Hugh O'Toole. 'And his wife – my sister, Róis, – the best brewer of ale this side of the Boyne. It will be lashings and leavings for all tonight, I'm thinking.'

Lashings and leavings! Hugh tried to imagine

himself snug and warm in Fiach's hall, with a mug of ale in his hand and a bowl of broth in front of him, but reality kept intruding. Before he could enjoy the hospitality of Ballinacor he had somehow to get himself there – and for the life of him he couldn't see how his feet were going to carry him.

Perhaps when I've rested a bit, he thought desperately. He stretched out on the soggy ground and the relief was almost intoxicating. I won't sleep, he promised himself, I'll just lie here till I get my strength back. But his eyes ached. In the end he had to close them – and suddenly Cormac's voice jolted him out of a dream, urging them all to their feet again.

He opened his eyes. It was full daylight now – though the clouds made it difficult to tell – and the rain was coming down more heavily than ever. He shivered and pulled his sodden cloak around him, Cormac had the truth of it – they had to keep moving. The English would be scouring the countryside for them by now. But . . . he closed his eyes again. Oh, God, for just a few more moments – a few precious seconds before he needed to walk again.

He felt a hand shaking him by the shoulder. 'Hugh,' said Donal's voice, 'Hugh, get up. We have to be going.'

Swaying like a drunk, he dragged himself to his feet. Donal stared at him anxiously. 'Are you all right?'

He nodded, but when he tried to take a step it was like walking on needles.

'Jesu!' exclaimed Donal. 'What's on you, Hugh Roe? Are you sick?'

He shook his head. 'My feet,' he croaked.

Donal lowered him to the ground and pulled off his tattered shoes. 'Holy Mother of God! Why didn't you tell us?' He lifted his voice. 'Cormac! Come here till you see this.'

Their guide turned and came hurrying back. Hugh looked down at his feet – blistered and bruised, bleeding from innumerable scratches. Panic seized him. He couldn't possibly walk as far as Glenmalure in this condition. What in the world was he to do?

He looked helplessly at his friends. Donal and Cormac looked at each other. 'Will we bandage them,' suggested Donal doubtfully.

'It might help.' Cormac pushed back his cloak and ripped off one of his voluminous shirt sleeves. 'Here,' he said, 'use this.'

Donal tore the linen into strips and he and Cormac set about bandaging Hugh's feet. Hugh felt very foolish. 'It is my own shirt you should be using,' he protested, but Cormac pretended not to hear.

'There now,' he said, when at last they were finished. 'Let's have you up now and see can you walk again.'

They helped him to his feet and, with his arms around their shoulders, set off again. For a while Hugh managed to ignore the pain, but it grew steadily worse. Before long they had to stop and let him rest again.

'This is hopeless,' he gasped, as they lowered him to the ground. 'You'll have to leave me here.'

'We'll do no such thing,' retorted Donal. 'Are we

Saxons to be turning our backs on one of our own?' He looked at his companions. 'We'll carry him if we have to, won't we, lads?'

'We will,' they agreed, but Hugh could see how worried Cormac looked. Time was slipping away and time was the one thing they did not have. Fitzwilliam would have search parties all over the mountains by now. How would he live with himself if they all got caught because of him? Donal had already been cheated of freedom once.

'You'll not carry me,' he said. 'I'll not let you. Leave me here in the shelter of these trees and send someone back for me when you reach Ballinacor.'

They looked at each other doubtfully. 'It might be safest,' admitted Cormac, 'for Hugh as well as for us. We've a rocky road ahead of us yet.'

'Then I'll stay with him,' said Donal.

'You will not,' said Hugh.

'Ah, try and stop me.'

They glowered at each other.

'Will you hold your row, the pair of you,' broke in Hugh O'Toole. 'Haven't I a better plan, entirely. We're only a mile or so from Castlekevin – my brother's stronghold. I can be there and back while a cat would be licking its paws and fetch help for Hugh Roe, while the rest of you go on to Glenmalure.'

They all turned to look at him. 'I know it's not as safe as Ballinacor,' he continued. 'But Felim will see us right. He promised us help at any time and we asking for it.'

'So he did,' agreed Hugh. 'And Felim O'Toole is a man of his word.'

Donal still looked unhappy. 'I don't like to split up the group,' he protested. 'Maybe we should all make for Castlekevin.'

Hugh shook his head. 'I'll not give Felim more trouble than I have to.'

'But someone should stay with you,' persisted Donal.

'Am I a child? I'll manage fine, and one man hiding among these trees will be harder to spot than two. Will you go now. Every minute you stand here, doesn't it bring the English closer?'

For a moment Donal looked as though he were going to argue, but at last he hunched his shoulders in a gesture of resignation. He leaned down and grasped Hugh's hand. 'God go with you, Hugh Roe. We'll celebrate together at Rathmullen.'

'We will, and Eoghan with us. God speed the journey, Donal.'

ten

HUGH WATCHED TILL his companions were out of sight, then settled down to await Hugh O'Toole's return. He had never felt more alone. The mountains were vast and alien. They were not his mountains, and they stretched out bewilderingly in all directions to horizons shrouded in mist and rain. He had no idea where he was. Which way was Castlekevin? Which way was Glenmalure? And would Hugh O'Toole find his way back to this spot, or would an English search party find the place before him?

Wet, hungry and chilled to the very marrow, Hugh huddled in his shelter beneath a clump of pines and pulled his cloak more tightly round his shoulders. The confidence he had pretended earlier shrivelled like a flower after frost. He didn't know which he feared more – being found by the English or not being found at all.

Above everything he longed to sleep. He didn't dare to close his eyes, but that didn't stop him dreaming – weird, hallucinatory nightmares: disembodied heads grinning down at him from the trees, and ghostly figures swirling about him in the rain. When he heard voices, he thought they too were part of the dream. It wasn't till they surrounded him that he realised they were Irish – and that one of them belonged to Hugh O' Toole.

They brought him down to Castlekevin on a litter. He remembered little of the journey – only the comfort of rugs, the voices of his rescuers and the utter bliss of knowing he was safe. At the hall they had prepared him a bed near the fire. Hands stripped him of his wet clothes and he sank into the mattress gratefully. Other hands – or maybe they were the same ones – bathed his feet. Voices spoke reassuringly. He was aware of it all – but only dimly, as if it were happening far away, to someone else. Soon even the faint echoes faded.

He woke in darkness, ravenously hungry. The fire was still flickering and he could hear voices nearby, arguing softly. One he recognised – it was Felim's. The other belonged to a woman. She seemed to be trying to reassure Felim. 'Will you stop your worrying,' she said. 'It is all in Fiach's hands now.'

'I know, but . . .'

'You are after doing everything you could. No one will blame you, whatever happens.'

'It's the weather I'm fearful for,' said Felim. 'With the rain that's in it . . .'

The sentence was left unfinished. Hugh turned his head to look at the speakers, but they were only shadows in the firelight. The rush mattress rustled as he moved and the woman must have heard it, for she stood up and came over to his bed. She was tall, with strong features and hair that glowed copper-coloured in the firelight. She put him in mind of his mother. He wondered who she was, but somehow it seemed impolite to ask.

She smiled down at him. 'So, awake at last. And with a hunger on you to eat an ox and I'm not mistaken?'

He nodded.

'I'll bring you something.'

She went away and returned with cold meat and cheese and a loaf of barley bread. It seemed to Hugh the most wonderful food he had ever tasted. He wolfed it down, while his hostess sat on the end of his mattress and watched him. Not till he had licked the last crumbs from his fingers did she speak again. 'So,' she said at last. 'The famous Hugh Roe O'Donnell. And yourself as welcome as the swallows to Castlekevin. My brother has told me much about you.'

'Your brother?'

'I am Róis O'Toole. Felim's sister.'

'Ah,' said Hugh. He remembered something else. 'And Fiach mac Hugh's wife.'

'For my sins!' She chuckled. 'And which of them the greater trouble to me, only the Dear knows.'

Hugh smiled. He looked across at Felim. 'God save you, Felim O'Toole, it's a generous man you are. Wouldn't I be dead by now and you not fetching me down off that mountain? But I fear I am after bringing you into danger.'

Felim and his sister exchanged glances. 'We are

honoured to have you, Hugh Roe,' said Róis quickly. 'And danger? – sure, don't we live with that every day? But Castlekevin is not safe for you and that's the truth of it. The road from Dublin comes almost to our door. The Lord Deputy's troops will seek you out here eventually as sure as Easter follows Lent.'

'Then I must go, as soon as it's light. I'll not have you arrested for hiding me.'

'Will you hold your peace and listen to what I'm telling you! We have it all planned out. Felim dare not openly defy the Lord Deputy. For the safety of his household, he is after sending a messenger to Dublin to tell them you are here. But –' she grinned – 'sure, wasn't it a very slow messenger, on a very lame horse; and in the meantime our Hugh is away like the wild hunt to Glenmalure, with news of your predicament. When the Lord Deputy's troops arrive here, they will learn that Fiach mac Hugh is after attacking Castlekevin and carrying you off by force to his own stronghold.'

Hugh shook his head. It was an ingenious plan, but far too dangerous. 'They'll not believe you. And what if they follow me to Ballinacor?'

Fiach's wife threw back her head and laughed. 'And they remembering what happened the last troop of Saxons who ventured into Glenmalure? They'd be the fools.' She stood up and took the empty plate from him. '"Bloody Monday", the English call that day – and Dublin still shaking in its shoes at the memory. Trust me – you will be safe with Fiach. Now, lie down and get your rest.

With luck he will be here at first light, and you must be ready to ride.'

Hugh obeyed. It was good to drift into sleep, knowing he was watched over and protected. Once during the night he woke to hear rain beating down on the thatch. Felim had spoken of rain. He had been worried about it – but why, what possible danger could it pose? He tried to think, but he was too sleepy and light-headed. This place was warm and comforting – nothing could touch him here.

When next he opened his eyes it was broad daylight. His hosts were nowhere to be seen, but someone had put out dry clothes for him and a pair of stout Irish boots. He crawled out of bed. Why had they let him sleep so long? At any moment Fiach mac Hugh would be here to take him to Ballinacor. Hastily he dressed himself.

He was easing his still tender feet into the new shoes when the door opened and Róis came in. He looked up. 'Is he here?'

She shook her head.

'Oh, I thought . . .' He broke off, staring at her. Something was wrong. Her face was white and strained. She looked as if she were about to cry. But that would be unthinkable. It would be like seeing his mother cry, and the Iníon Dubh, he was positive, was incapable of tears. He felt a prickle of fear. 'What is it?' he whispered. 'Tell me what is wrong.'

'Ah, Hugh.' She had control of herself again – only the catch in her voice betrayed her pain. 'It's the rain, son – all that rain last night.'

'What do you mean?' He could hear her words, he could see a vague black shape of danger behind them, but his mind could not put it into focus. 'What do you mean, the rain?' he asked again.

'The river – the Annamoe. With the rain that's in it, isn't it in flood and every ford impassable?'

This couldn't be happening. He felt a cold fist tighten round his heart. 'But . . . but surely there is some other path?'

'My sorrow, there is not. There is no path between here and Glenmalure that does not cross the river.'

'And . . .' his voice was a whisper, 'and to Dublin?'

She looked at him as though her heart would break. 'Ah, *mo chroí*, there is no river crosses the road to Dublin.'

● ● ●

He had a meal – Róis insisted he should eat – and then they waited. The hours crawled by, like flies dragging themselves through honey. Instinct urged him to run – but how far could he hope to get in his present state? And what punishment might Fitzwilliam inflict on Felim O'Toole for allowing such a prize catch to slip through his fingers. In the silence, he remembered something old Gráinne O'Malley had once said – and she a guest at Donegal. How on a luckless voyage, a sailor might come on deck one morning and know by the winds and the set of the tide that his ship would be driven on the rocks that night – and he with no recourse but to watch and wait for it to happen. Hugh felt like the master of that vessel. Apart from Róis, none of Felim's household came near him – not even Felim himself. It was as though no one could bear to look him in the face.

Just after midday, he heard the horses. He scrambled to his feet. Róis rose also. She put a hand on his arm. 'Courage, Hugh. Be strong.'

He felt himself shivering.

The riders drew up outside the hall. He heard the murmur of voices. Then the door burst open and a big, florid man in English clothes strode into the room, flanked by half a dozen soldiers. Felim O'Toole was behind them. Felim looked at Hugh. 'I'm sorry, son. This is Sir George Carew. He is come –'

But the Englishman was already striding forward. 'So, Master O'Donnell,' he jeered, 'run to earth like a fox, eh? And a merry chase you and your friends have led us. I wouldn't be in your shoes when we get you back to Dublin.' He hooked his thumbs into his belt and grinned at his prisoner. 'And where are your friends?'

Hugh said nothing. Carew jabbed him in the chest with one finger. 'Answer me, you little guttersnipe.'

'Where you'll never get your stinking hands on them.'

Carew struck him across the face. He staggered backwards and before he could recover his balance, the Englishman hit him again. This time, he fell. As he struggled to his feet, Carew raised his fist for another blow, but Róis stepped between them. 'You are wasting your time, my Lord. The boy has no idea where his friends are. They left him for dead in the mountains and it's only by the grace of God we found him.'

Carew looked at Hugh. 'Is that the truth?'

'It's all you'll get.'

'God's death, boy, you try me too far!' For a moment Hugh thought the man was going to strike him again, but then he seemed to change his mind. His fists uncurled and he laughed – a chilling sound. 'No matter,' he said 'They'll have the truth out of you in Dublin.' He turned to his men. 'Take him outside and put him on a horse. And make sure his feet are chained. He may have made a fool of the Constable but, by God, he'll not slip through *my* fingers.'

The soldiers closed round him. On of them gave him a shove in the back. 'Move,' he said.

Hugh straightened. His hands felt clammy. The muscles in his jaw quivered, tight as the skin on a drum. He looked at Róis and she stared back at him fiercely. Walk, he told himself, hold your head up and walk, don't give them the satisfaction of dragging you out. He took one step, then another, fighting the panic that urged him to break and run. Prickles of pain ran through his feet. He knew Carew was watching him: he could feel the Englishman's gaze burning a hole in his back. He took another step, and then – Carew laughed.

Hugh snapped.

With a wild cry, he flung aside his escort and bolted through the door. His legs pumped – driving him almost of their own accord. Pain washed up from his feet in burning waves. There was nowhere to go, nowhere to hide, but he could not let them take him. He would freeze in the mountains, drown in the Annamoe before they dragged him back to Dublin.

He heard yelling behind him, hoof beats. Out of the corner of his eye he saw a horse bearing down on him. He ran faster. A hand reached down and grabbed him by the collar. He was lifted, dragged, dropped again outside the hall. He lay in the dirt, sobbing helplessly.

There was a silence. 'Get him on his feet,' commanded Carew's voice. Footsteps approached, but it was Róis O'Toole who dropped to her knees beside him. It was Róis who wiped the tears and dirt from his face; whose arms held him; whose voice whispered in his ear.

'Fight them, Hugh, fight them. Don't let them break your spirit.'

But he couldn't. He clung to her as a drowning man clings to a rope. 'I can't, Róis. I'll rot and die in that stinking castle.'

'You will not.' Her hands were strong about his shoulders, her voice rang like a bell. 'You will survive, and the English queen will curse the day she ever laid hands on you. You are Hugh, son of Hugh – the prophesied one of the Cenél Chonaill. You were not born to die in an English prison.'

He shivered. What was she saying? Her hands gripped till they hurt, her eyes stared into the distance. Words flashed across Hugh's mind: *'When Hugh succeeds Hugh . . . the last Hugh shall be Ard Rígh of all Ireland and drive all the foreigners out.*' Was that what she meant? Did she, Róis O'Toole, see something that he could not see?

He gulped. 'Second sight'. It was an awesome thought – as terrifying, in its way, as the thought of going back to Dublin – and yet, it gave him back his courage. Only time would reveal the truth of her prophecy. But one thing he could not deny: he was Hugh Roe O'Donnell, chieftain's son of the Cenél Chonaill, and he must keep faith with his father's people. An O'Donnell did not grovel before his foes.

'Let me up,' he whispered.

She released him. He rose to his feet. He could feel the steely strength of her will supporting him. With his head high and his body rigid as a pikestaff, he went forward towards his enemies.

eleven

THE JOURNEY BACK to Dublin felt to Hugh like a funeral procession – a journey to the graveyard, and himself nailed down in the coffin, still alive. He tried to feed his courage on Róis's prophetic words, but it was hard to feel confident surrounded by your enemies, with chains on your hands and feet and the reins of your horse given into the keeping of one of your captors. Carew's threat kept coming back to him. 'I wouldn't be in your shoes when we get you back to Dublin.' What would they do to him? Fitzwilliam, facing the wrath of his queen, must be furious. And Maplesdene, the new Constable who had replaced Seagar some eighteen months earlier, was not a man to forgive easily either. As they rode over the castle bridge, Hugh looked up at the trophies above the gate and knew a moment of sheer terror.

In the courtyard, Carew dismounted and swaggered off to report his success to the Lord Deputy, leaving his prisoner in the charge of the Constable. 'And kennel him securely,' Carew said. 'I have better things to do than chase round the countryside after runaway puppies.'

Maplesdene looked at Hugh grimly. 'He'll not slip his leash again,' he promised. He flicked a hand at the guards. 'Take him away and lock him up.'

Without ceremony, Hugh was dragged from his horse and hustled across the courtyard – not back to the gatetower, as he had hoped, but to another building next to the hall. Through a door he was led, and down many flights of stairs, till at last he found himself in a long, dank corridor. It was cold and dark, lit only by a few torches set in sconces in the stone. Little runnels of water trickled down its walls.

His captors slid back the bolt on a thick, iron-studded door. Beyond it Hugh saw a tiny cell – a stone vault, hardly bigger than a tomb. It was dark and damp; its walls were slippery; it stank like a duck pond. It was the dungeon of his worst fears.

He shrank back. A hand shoved him in the back and he stumbled into the vault. The door slammed. A bolt thudded home. He was alone in utter blackness. He crawled into a corner and sat there, his knees hunched to his chin, fighting hysteria, straining his eyes for some glimpse of his surroundings. A minute sliver of light, thrown by the torches in the corridor, crept underneath the door, but it was not strong enough to relieve the blackness – only to add deeper, grotesque shapes to its depths.

He tried to retreat into memories – those delirious hours of liberty: the smell of rain on the mountains, the fireside at Castlekevin, the strong, motherly arms of Róis

O'Toole. But each time his mind wandered. Coldness, or some sick, unearthly sound from beyond his tomb, would jolt him back to reality. The darkness began to worm its way into his bones. Occasionally he did drift into sleep, but his dreams were so ghost-ridden it was almost a relief to wake again.

It was impossible to judge the passing of time. It might have been hours, it might have been days before the door opened at last and one of his jailers entered the cell.

'Out!'

Hugh was in no state to argue. Stumbling and half blinded by the sudden light, he allowed himself to be hustled back along the corridor and into another room – a long, stone-flagged hall. Four soldiers guarded the door – two outside, two inside. Others were posted around the walls. A fire flickered in a brazier in the centre of the floor, and there was a table where things of iron were laid out in rows – implements at whose function he could only guess. The room was cold despite the brazier, and it stank of something undefinable – sweat or stale urine or . . . or blood.

They will have the truth out of you in Dublin.

Fight, screamed his mind. *Run.* But his body was powerless, frozen like a wild duck caught in the ice of a winter pond.

The guards stripped him, dragged him across the room and shackled him, spread-eagled, to iron rings set in the wall. Too late, panic galvanised him and he began to struggle. He sobbed and cursed and wrenched at his bonds till his wrists and ankles bled, but it was a waste of time. When exhaustion had finally brought him to a standstill, he lifted his head and saw that the Constable had come into the room.

Maplesdene looked at him in silence for a long time. 'Well, Master O'Donnell,' he said at last, 'you see how little your foolish efforts have availed you. Now you have some accounting to do.'

Hugh shuddered. He wanted so desperately to be brave – to spit in the man's face and shout defiance at him – but he couldn't. He knew if he uttered one word he would be done for. He would weep and plead and babble like a child and tell them everything they wished to know. Other men – older, stronger men than he – had marched into this room arrogant in their courage, and crawled out broken and submissive. What hope was there for him where they had failed? He was not heroic. Any courage he might have possessed had died in the darkness of his dungeon.

'Where are your friends?' demanded Maplesdene.

He shut his eyes.

A fist thudded into his face. 'Irish filth! Answer the Constable when he speaks to you.'

His head cracked against the wall. He gasped and spat blood from his bitten tongue. His eyes focused slowly on Maplesdene. The Constable was watching him, appraising him, despising him for his cowardice. Shame almost drowned out his terror. And then, in a blinding flash, the truth hit him. It didn't matter! This wasn't about his courage or dignity. It was about lives – Dick Weston's, Róis's, Hugh mac Ferdoragh's. He did not have to be brave, all he had to be was silent.

They hammered him with questions – 'Who helped you?' 'Who brought you rope?' 'Who guided you?' 'What part did the Earl of Tyrone play?' – and each time he refused to speak, they beat him again. His ribs cracked, his legs buckled, white lights exploded inside his head. He sobbed, screamed, vomited repeatedly. But not one coherent word escaped his lips.

Finally there was a pause and a voice said in English, 'We waste our efforts, my Lord. The brat has all the impudence of Satan. Shall I heat the irons?'

Hot irons! Worms of terror crawled through Hugh's guts. There was a ghastly silence. Then Maplesdene's voice said peevishly, 'No. Throw him back in his cell. Cold and hunger will loosen his tongue soon enough.'

He had won, but it didn't feel like a victory. The fetters were unlocked and he collapsed on the flagstones. Hands jerked him to his feet and half dragged, half carried him back to his cell. He lay where they dropped him. Iron rattled as they shackled his wrists and ankles. The door closed, plunging him back into darkness.

The cold was the worst part. He was still naked and there was nothing in the cell with which to cover himself. Dampness crept into every fibre of his body. Sleep was impossible, except for stray moments of exhaustion, and even then the cold followed him into his dreams. He saw the dead Spaniards – the men of the *Trinidad Valencera* – stripped naked and hunted across the bog by their murderers. Their white bodies drifted round him, pale as ghosts. Their dark, corpse-like eyes stared at him hungrily. 'A life for a life,' they seemed to say. 'A death for a death.' There was a terrible logic to it.

Am I in hell? he wondered. The priests, in their sermons, always described it as a fire – but they were wrong. Hell was cold. Hell was a dark crypt, where water dripped down the walls and light never penetrated and blackness froze the marrow in your bones. Hell was a dungeon beneath Dublin Castle.

Day and night became meaningless. Every now and then someone brought food and asked was he ready to answer questions. When he said nothing, they took it away again. After a while he did not care. He was wandering further and further from reality. The cold was interspersed with bouts of raging heat and he no longer knew when he slept or when he woke.

It came to him that he was dying. How bold of him. The Lord Deputy would be outraged, and Róis O'Toole – would she ever forgive him for bringing all her fine prophecies to nothing? He should go to her, tell her he was sorry; but it was such a long way to Castlekevin, and he had no energy for walking.

A voice from far away broke through his delirium – the same wearisome, English voice. 'Well, brat, are you disposed to be reasonable yet?'

He ignored it – soon it would go away again.

A foot prodded him in the ribs. 'Go to, Master O'Donnell, you cannot sulk for ever. Eventually you will have to eat.'

He rolled his head away from the sound.

'I mislike this,' said the first voice. 'He looks sick to me.'

There was a laugh. 'Nah, he is just moping. They're all the same, these so-called Irish princes – put them in chains and they whimper like beaten curs.'

'Even so . . .' A hand touched his face. 'God's blood, he's burning up with fever. Fetch the Constable, quickly.'

There was a confusion of activity – feet, voices, ebbing and flowing like the ripples on Lough Swilly. Water was put to his lips, something warm was wrapped round his shoulders. 'Bring him out of there,' ordered a voice he recognised, and hands fumbled at his wrists and ankles. He wanted to laugh. How did Maplesdene expect to revive him now – *order* him to get well again? You're too late, he thought wearily. I'm after cheating you.

Two sets of hands hoisted him to his feet, but he couldn't stand – his body was all arms and legs and none of them worked properly. He looked down and saw himself from a distance, dangling naked between them like an injured heron; and then he blacked out.

He was warm and lying in a bed. He shouldn't be there, but he couldn't remember why and the effort was wearisome. The warmth seduced him. It ran through his veins like whiskey. He lay in a cocoon, lapping it up as a cat laps up cream. Presently he slept, and when he woke there was a face looking down at him. A round, Irish face – a face that seemed to wish him well. It smiled at him, and he smiled back, vaguely aware that he had not the faintest idea who it belonged to. 'God save you,' he mumbled.

The plump features creased with laughter. '"God save you," indeed. And a fine greeting that is, to be sure, from one returned almost from the dead. Didn't we think it was burying you we'd be?'

'We?' even as he formed the question, a second voice chimed in from somewhere out of sight. 'And no great loss either,' it growled. 'Is it ourselves to be keening for an O'Donnell?'

The friendly face turned away. 'Ah, shut your gob, Henry. What harm is the lad after doing you? Save your anger for the Saxons.'

The unseen Henry muttered something incomprehensible. His companion turned back to Hugh. 'You must excuse my brother,' he grinned. 'Didn't he get out on the wrong side of his bed this morning.'

Hugh's head began to spin. None of this was making any sense. Where was he? How had he got here? Who were these two men, one of whom seemed to dislike him so heartily? 'Do I know you?' he asked at last.

The round-faced man laughed. 'You do,' he said, 'though, in truth, I think you never saw me before. I am Art mac Shane, and the bull with the bad manners over there, is my brother Henry.'

Art and Henry mac Shane! Shane O'Neill's sons! The mortal enemies of both The O'Donnell and Hugh mac Ferdoragh! Hugh stared at the man, dumbfounded. Art chuckled. 'Rest easy, Hugh Roe. I bear you no ill will, for all that you are an O'Donnell.' He leaned closer and the corner of his mouth twitched in a wry grin. 'After all, isn't it cousins we are – you and I – in a manner of speaking?'

In a manner of speaking! Hugh shuddered, remembering the story. Thirty-odd years ago it was, after another clash in the traditional O'Donnell–O'Neill feud. His uncle Calvagh O'Donnell lying prisoner in Shane O'Neill's dungeons, and Shane upstairs in his bedchamber with Calvagh's wife. Hugh looked at Art mac Shane – the product of that shameful coupling – and tried to think of something to say, but it was beyond him. Blood sang in his ears. Art's face danced before his eyes. He felt himself sliding back into darkness.

He slept on and off for most of that day, waking only to eat and drink. From time to time, a little man whom Art said was the apothecary, scuttled in like a frightened crab to fuss over him and give him cordials. Hugh tried to piece together what had happened.

'How long am I after lying here?' he asked Art. 'I . . . I don't remember . . . Did I have a fever?'

'A fever!' Art chuckled. 'Mother of God, will you listen while I tell you. Three days ago they brought you in here – and you with a fire in your head fit to bake bread on. Three days, muttering and moaning and threshing around on that bed, and Maplesdene in and out, roaring like a bull and putting the fear of death into your man there, and he not keeping you alive.'

Memories began to filter back. Hugh shuddered. 'I wonder they did not let me die,' he said bitterly.

'Ha! And you the best pledge on all Tír Chonaill – are they the fools? Small value they'd gain from a dead hostage.'

'More's the pity,' chipped in Henry mac Shane caustically.

Art turned on his brother. 'Ah, will you hold your tongue, Henry, haven't we troubles enough without fighting among ourselves?' He winked at Hugh. 'Ignore him. It's as sour as a sorrel leaf he is at the whole world, and it's not this week or last it happened him. It's my belief he is not after forgiving his mother yet for giving birth to him without his permission.'

Hugh had to smile. Despite everything, he was beginning to like this plump, good-natured man. Prison made a mockery of freedom's quarrels. The enemy of my enemy is my friend, and could Art help it if his father had been a monster?

Henry was easier to dislike. He was surly by nature and imprisonment seemed to have brought out the worst in him. He snarled at everyone – even his own brother – and appeared to hold Art responsible for their present misfortunes. Art had escaped briefly the previous year and since then, both brothers had been made to wear leg irons.

Hugh could understand Henry's anger – keeping a

man in chains was about the greatest humiliation you could inflict on him; but to blame Art seemed grossly unfair. Wouldn't Henry have tried to escape, and he having the opportunity? Hugh lay on his sick-bed and watched them bickering, and wondered what the future held in store for himself.

As soon as he was strong enough to walk again, Maplesdene ordered that he, too, should be put in chains. It was a crushing blow, even though he had expected it, and he was hard put not to struggle as the fetters were locked round his ankles. He looked afresh round his new lodgings and his heart sank. This was a far cry from the room he had shared with Eoghan and Donal in the gate-tower. It was large enough – it even had its own privy in a small side chamber – but the windows were all barred and the door permanently locked. For all its size, this room was a prison cell.

'Do they never let you out?' he asked Art fearfully.

The older man smiled. 'Ah, they do,' he said kindly. 'They let us take exercise in the courtyard every now and then.'

'And . . . and these?' Hugh looked down at his leg irons.

Art shook his head.

It was hard to sleep with chains on your feet. Tossing and turning on his straw in the underground cell to which they were removed each night, Hugh recalled with bitterness

Róis O'Toole's brave prophecy. How little she had known. All the magic of the otherworld would not spirit him out of this place.

In the darkness he could hear Art and Henry talking. Henry was grumbling as usual, but Art, for some reason, seemed buoyed up with optimism. 'Will you leave the lad be,' he told his brother. 'Hasn't he friends working even now to break him out. And where one goes others may follow – I'm telling you he may yet be the saving of us.'

'Ha! And when the sky falls we'll all catch larks. Why do you think Fitzwilliam is after foisting him on us?'

'What do you mean?'

'Think man, who engineered his last escape?'

'Doesn't everyone know it was Hugh mac Ferdoragh? And . . .'

'And Hugh mac Ferdoragh is as crafty as a fox. He may want O'Donnell's son out of prison, but there is one thing he wants even more – and that's his own foot on the inauguration stone of the O'Neills when old Turlough Luineach dies. And who are the men best placed to thwart that hope – and they safe back in Ulster again?'

'*Chreesta*! You mean . . .'

Henry mac Shane laughed maliciously. 'I'm telling you, Art, Fitzwilliam is after chaining this brat to us like a donkey to a cart. It will be an icy day in hell before Hugh mac Ferdoragh gives a means of escape to anyone and he to be sharing it with the sons of Shane O'Neill?'

twelve

THREE THOUSAND POUNDS,' said the Earl of Tyrone. 'Think about it. It is a great deal of money.'

He cupped his wine glass in his hands and swirled the contents gently. His eyes smiled over the rim at the Lord Deputy. Fitzwilliam shifted uncomfortably. Every instinct warned him to stop this conversation before it went any further, but Hugh mac Ferdoragh O'Neill was a hard man to deny. He was charming and persuasive; his voice had the smoothness of warm honey – and what he had said was the truth, three thousand pounds was indeed a very great deal of money.

'And a man in your position . . .' continued O'Neill. He smiled again and did not finish the sentence. He did not need to. They both knew very well what he meant. Everything cost money in this wretched country. Supplies, information – even loyalty – had to be bought. A Lord Deputy without money was a Lord Deputy without power, and Fitzwilliam was not a wealthy man.

Why didn't they understand that in London? Time

and again he had begged for more resources. But even after the Armada – even after he had personally saved this miserable island of hers from hordes of marauding Spaniards – the queen still had not appreciated his worth. 'Reward?' she had thundered, when he made his modest submission. 'Must we remind you, Sir William, that the post of Lord Deputy is a preferment, not a service. There are others who would be only too eager to accept the honour, should you wish to surrender it.' After all he had done for her! It was bitterly unjust. He felt his face twist into a scowl.

'They do, indeed, treat you shamefully,' murmured O'Neill, almost as though he could read his thoughts. 'I, on the other hand, am generous to those who accommodate me. And I do not even ask you to free the young man – only to move him to a more . . . shall we say . . . congenial prison.'

And one from which he could escape without the encumbrance of the Mac Shanes! Fitzwilliam was not a fool. He knew what would be expected of him when the time came. Nevertheless, it was tempting – three thousand pounds was a small fortune and the brat had always been more trouble than he was worth. But the risk . . . 'They would have my head,' he murmured.

'Ah, well!' O'Neill shrugged. 'If you have no stomach for it . . . But hostages have escaped before and no blame falling on the Lord Deputy. No prison is utterly secure. Jailers pass in and out – can they all be trusted? And the lad is still permitted visitors.' His eyes narrowed, fixing

Fitzwilliam with a steady gaze. 'They tell me your Constable is unwell. Sick men sometimes make errors.'

Again Fitzwilliam wavered. The man was right, mistakes did happen, prisoners *did* escape; and it was true, Maplesdene had been unwell for some time now. If the old fool grew negligent in his illness and young O'Donnell slipped through his guard again, could anyone suspect the Lord Deputy of complicity?

'And both The O'Donnell and his wife would know whom to thank for their son's freedom,' suggested Tyrone. 'So would the young man himself.'

That was something he had never considered. The O'Donnell in his debt, the Scottish she-dragon eating from his hand – Fitzwilliam's imagination took flight. Why, Tír Chonaill would be his to command. He would be doing the state a favour. And three thousand pounds . . . He smiled. He was on the very point of saying yes – but then, just in time, he remembered something else. He recalled his interviews with O'Donnell's son. Submission? Gratitude? In a pig's ear! That red-headed brat didn't know the meaning of the words. He embodied all the perversity of his accursed race.

Exasperation swept over him. What made the Irish so intractable? One could bend over backwards to be charitable to them, yet they remained wilfully entrenched in sedition and arrogance. Loose Red Hugh O'Donnell? – it would be like loosing wildfire on the country.

He looked at his visitor and a little shiver ran down his back. How close he had come to forgetting. He saw afresh that the Earl of Tyrone was probably the most dangerous man in Ireland. Young O'Donnell wore his barbarism like a flag, but O'Neill had all the trappings of civilisation. He spoke English, he dressed in civilised clothes, his hair and beard were neatly clipped after the English fashion. His manners were elegant and his big hands toyed with his goblet as delicately as any courtier's. He was so nearly the English gentleman. It was only now and then, when his guard was down, that something gave him away. It might be the merest gesture – a facial expression, a flicker in the eyes – but if one looked closely enough the veneer would fall away and one would see what lay behind it: that primitive, untamed *otherness* that infected all the native Irish and that no amount of kindness or coercion could ever eradicate.

Fitzwilliam thanked God for his narrow escape. 'I am sorry,' he said firmly. 'I will continue to petition Her Majesty for the release of your young kinsman, but I will not – I dare not – connive at his escape. Hugh Roe O'Donnell will remain in the Bermingham Tower, and Art and Henry mac Shane will bear him company.'

'And that was his final word,' Hugh mac Ferdoragh said sadly. 'He was immovable – and I blue in the face from arguing.' He looked round the little group assembled in the hall of Rathmullen Castle and made a small gesture of helplessness.

There was a silence while his audience digested his

words. 'He fears for his own skin,' said The MacSweeney Fanad at last. 'And, faith, who wouldn't, with yon old red Morrigu breathing down his neck? So, what is to be done now?'

'For the moment – nothing. There is nothing we can do and he in the company of the Mac Shanes. For I dare not . . .'

'Dare not?' There was a roar from the end of the table. The Iníon Dubh came to her feet, her eyes blazing. 'God damn you, Hugh mac Ferdoragh. God damn you and you a gutless coward. My son, my beautiful Hugh Roe, lies rotting still in that stinking castle, chained like a criminal and sharing a cell with the hell-spawn of that monster, Shane O'Neill, and you tell me you dare not help him?'

'A coward, is it?' O'Neill also came to his feet. 'By God, woman, those words would be your last and I not a guest in this hall.'

'Ha! An empty threat. I am after sending better men than you to their graves.'

'Will you sit down and hold your peace, the pair of you,' ordered The MacSweeney. 'Whose cause does it serve but the Lord Deputy's and we fighting among ourselves? Can we not discuss this without quarrelling?'

The two adversaries scowled at each other. For a moment neither moved, but at last they both, reluctantly, resumed their seats. 'The Earl of Tyrone may do as he pleases,' sneered the Iníon Dubh. 'But if he will not help us, there are others who will. I'll go to Scotland. I'll hire mercenaries – I'll lead them to Dublin myself – before I'll see a child of mine eat his heart out in an English prison.'

Hugh mac Ferdoragh raised one eyebrow. 'Very touching. Your devotion to your eldest son does you credit – but weren't you quick enough, two years ago, to offer his brother in exchange for him?'

'I offered cattle, too. What signs of them did you see in Dublin? There is a wealth of difference between promise and intent.'

They continued to glower at each other, then suddenly Hugh mac Ferdoragh put his head back and laughed. 'Ah, you're a fine, fierce woman, Finnoula McDonnell. Another Maeve of Connaught and you holding Tír Chonaill together against all the odds these three years or more.' He spread his hands, palms upward. 'God knows, if there were any way . . . I love that boy almost as dearly as you do, but –'

'Spare me your pity,' said the Iníon Dubh coldly, 'and look more closely at your own danger. You need my son. You will never call yourself O'Neill without help from Tír Chonaill, and The O'Donnell, God save him, is senile now and little better than a prisoner in Donegal. What will happen when he dies?'

The man did not answer.

'You do not know? Well, let me tell you then. Before his corpse is cold, Niall Garbh and Hugh mac Hugh Dubh will be at each other like a pair of stags and every man who ever dreamed of putting his foot on the stone will start hiring mercenaries. The English will play one off against the other, just as they did in Monaghan, and . . . and . . .' her voice faltered as she struggled to control it. 'And Hugh Roe O'Donnell will go the same way as Hugh Roe mac Mahon.'

The others stared at her. 'God Almighty,' breathed MacSweeney. 'You don't really believe they would execute him?'

'Why not?'

'But he is a prisoner – a hostage in their care – what reason could they give?'

'None that they could not invent to suit their purposes. Or he might meet with a convenient *accident* – fall from a window and he trying to escape, or drown in the moat.'

And so he might – easily. There was a chilly silence. The Iníon Dubh looked at Hugh mac Ferdoragh. 'And here is something else I'll tell you for nothing. As long as Art and Henry mac Shane remain in Dublin Castle your position will never be secure.'

'Why do you say that?'

'Isn't it obvious? What Fitzwilliam holds he can loose – at any time he chooses – and with a company of English soldiers at their heels to march against you and back their claim to the chieftaincy.'

O'Neill chewed his lip.

'But if they escaped, now, and you abetting them, where could they run to but back to Ulster? Have you not prisons – or thorn trees – enough in Dungannon to take care of them?'

'Thorn trees!' The allusion was so blatant even MacSweeney gasped.

Hugh O'Neill only chuckled, however. 'Ah, and well you know it was no thorn tree,' he protested. 'Hugh Gavelach mac Shane was legally executed – and I miles away at the time.'

'That is as may be. Nevertheless, he is dead, and what happened one brother may easily happen them all. It's a long, rocky road from Dublin to Ulster.'

Hugh mac Ferdoragh shook his head. *Chreesta*, he thought, this woman has a mind like a dagger. He turned her words over in his head. She had the truth of it. The mac Shanes would be far less troublesome in his own keeping – and if he had the guiding of their escape . . . As she said, it was a long way from Dublin to Dungannon – anything might happen on the road. As for Hugh Roe – again, his mother was right. Without him, there would be chaos when old Hugh Dubh died and Turlough Luineach would take advantage of the upheavals.

No, a strong and friendly Tír Chonaill was crucial to his own survival – wasn't it for that he was after marrying The O'Donnell's daughter? Her recent death had weakened that alliance. Maybe he should think about forging another.

'He is my son-in-law,' he had told Walsingham when making his first plea for Hugh Roe's release. Perhaps the time had come to turn that lie into reality. He looked round the table. 'Very well,' he conceded. 'I will try again to get him out.'

'I knew you'd not desert us.' The Iníon Dubh flashed him a look of mingled triumph and gratitude. But even as he returned her smile he felt his heart sinking. Talk was easy, but how was the thing to be done? She hadn't seen that room in the Bermingham Tower. Money might buy rope – it might even unlock fetters – but what use was that and every window barred?

He sat in silence groping for ideas. His mind walked every square inch of Hugh Roe's prison – counted every stud in the door, every stone in the walls. He could see no chink, no weakness anywhere. And then he remembered something. He began to laugh and his companions looked at him, startled. '*Chreesta*, but it might work,' he said, half to himself. 'Isn't it the one thing they'd never think of.'

❀ ❀ ❀

'The privy!' snorted Henry mac Shane. 'He expects us to climb down the privy?'

'Will you keep your voice down,' hissed Art. He glanced at the young serving lad who had brought them the letter. 'Do you want to have all the guards in – and your man there after risking his life for us?'

Henry's scowl deepened. 'And how do we know we can trust him?' he jeered. 'Anyone can devise a letter. How do we know it's not an English trap?'

The young man flushed angrily. 'I am an O'Byrne,' he said, 'clansman to Fiach mac Hugh of Ballinacor. The O'Byrnes do not practise deceit.'

'Then why would one of them be serving in an

English castle – fetching and carrying for Saxons?'

'Why else but to gather information. Fiach mac Hugh has ears and eyes in many places where he cannot go himself.'

Henry mac Shane sniffed disbelievingly but his brother nodded. 'I believe you,' he said. 'A shrewd man, is the Raven of Glenmalure.'

'And the letter is genuine,' added Hugh, whisking it out of Henry's grasp and studying it again himself. 'That is Hugh mac Ferdoragh's hand, and his seal – I'd know them anywhere.'

'And he offering us a way out of this stinking hole,' said Art. 'What the devil is on you, Henry? You don't have to like the man, but–'

'I don't trust him, and no more should you. Why would he do anything for us, and he after murdering our brother?'

'He wouldn't – you have the truth of it – but he'd do it for Hugh Roe; and we to profit from his company.'

'Ha!' snorted Henry, and then, determined to have the last word: 'And isn't he after taking long enough about it.'

Art and Hugh smiled. Hugh read through the letter again. He could hardly take it in. A rope, a guide, horses to carry them to Glenmalure – could it be possible? He tried not to dream – not to allow himself to hope. Last year's nightmare was still etched into his memory. He looked at the messenger. 'How . . .' he began, but the lad shook his head.

'Don't ask. When the time comes you will have everything you need.' He grinned. 'I'll not be back myself, but there will be others – I am not the only ears and eyes about this castle.' And he went out, locking the door ostentatiously behind him.

The three young men stared at each other. There seemed nothing adequate to say. Then Henry broke the silence. 'But down the privy,' he wailed. '*Chreesta*, I'll come out stinking like a turd.'

Hugh bit back the obvious retort.

❈ ❈ ❈

During the Christmas holiday, the letter had promised. For the next two weeks the hostages waited anxiously, but there was no further message. Hugh's confidence began to wane. Something must have gone wrong, he thought despondently. He didn't say anything to the others but he didn't need to – Henry was vocal enough for all of them.

Then, on Christmas Eve just before supper-time, two of Maplesdene's minions carried a chest into the room. 'For Master O'Donnell,' they announced. 'A gift from his mother, the Iníon Dubh, which the Lord Deputy has graciously consented to his receiving.' Hugh tried not to stare at it – or at his friends. He was terrified the guards would read his thoughts. But the moment they had gone, the three prisoners fell on the chest and flung the lid open.

There was a long silence as they stared at the contents. Then: 'Bed linen!' exploded Henry. 'Nothing but stupid sheets and coverlets!' He rummaged in the chest like a dog digging in sand and tossed linen about the room disgustedly. 'What did I tell you?' he crowed bitterly. 'It was all talk. He's after abandoning us.'

'Is there even a note in there?' asked Art, not sounding very hopeful.

There was, but the seal had been broken and there was no word in it unfit for English scrutiny. It merely expressed the Lady O'Donnell's affection for her son, urged him to maintain his courage and hoped he would have good usage from her gift. Hugh read it and handed it silently to Art. He could not bring himself to speak. Henry was right. It had all been talk. There would be no escape. The Iníon Dubh was a canny woman – a Scot – she would not be after sending him a gift and she knowing he would never use it.

'Bed linen!' jeered Henry again. 'And is it fine feather beds she thinks we have in that cell we sleep in?' He scrunched one of the sheets into a ball and threw it at Hugh. 'The only good you'll have from that is to use it in the privy.'

'The what?' Hugh stared at him. A light flickered in his mind. He looked at the sheet, then at Art. They both turned to look at Henry.

'Ah, no,' said Henry, realisation slowly dawning on him. 'Ah, no – it can't be.'

But it could. 'And we the fools not to be thinking of it before,' said Art. 'What did your man say? "You'll have everything you need when the time comes".' And he began to laugh.

Hugh wanted to laugh as well – and to cry and shout and sing, all at the same time. His heart felt wrung out – torn between new hope and the terror of disillusionment. Only Henry remained sceptical. 'And what about these?' he demanded, sitting on a chair and waggling his leg irons at his companions.

Art laughed louder. 'When the time comes, remember? Have faith, you great *amadán*.' He began to gather up the linen and stuff it back into the chest. 'And now let's get this stuff out of sight before they come to fetch us away to our supper.'

Over the next few days they tore the linen into strips and knotted them together. They took turns, one keeping an ear to the door while the others worked, and the finished rope was coiled neatly back in the chest, hidden by a coverlet.

'Will it hold our weight, do you think?' asked Art anxiously.

Henry looked at his brother. 'Sure, it will hold me well enough, and Hugh Roe here has no more meat on him than a raven's bit. But we'll send you down last, I'm thinking, Art, just to be on the safe side – and I wouldn't be eating anything between then and now and I were you.'

Art smiled, but it was plain the jibe had hurt him. Hugh felt angry. Art wasn't fat, just a little on the plump side; and if he was slow and clumsy, wasn't it from the wounds he had received fighting to avoid recapture after his last escape? Hugh added another spike to the grievance he was nursing against Henry mac Shane.

Once the rope was finished, there was nothing to do but wait. The anticipation nearly drove them mad. One by one, the twelve days of Christmas came and went and never a word from their would-be rescuer. They began to grow restless and to question their optimism. Had they made a mistake? Had hope caused their imaginations to run away with them? Henry began grumbling again and Hugh found it hard to keep his temper. Even Art was morose and fidgety.

On the afternoon of the eleventh day – the eve of the Epiphany – they were taken down to the courtyard for exercise. The castle was still in holiday mood and in the stableyard some of the young horseboys had started an impromptu hurling match. Hugh watched them enviously. How often had he engaged in similar romps at Castle Doe with his foster brothers. Freedom had been something he took for granted then. How could he have imagined it would all end like this? Even walking in leg irons was an effort.

Depressed, he sat down on a low wall to watch the game. Most of the garrison seemed to have turned out, too, and there was a lot of good-natured cat-calling going on. 'What team would you have your money on?' Art shouted in his ear, but he only shrugged. It was all one to him.

The game see-sawed up and down the yard, with neither side able to gain the upper hand. Then, suddenly, one of the players made a wild slash with his stick that sent the ball hurtling out of play and smack into the wall beneath Hugh's feet. Half a dozen youngsters dashed over to retrieve it. There was a wild scrimmage and in the midst of it one of the players managed to get his stick tangled in Hugh's chains. Almost before the boy realised what was happening, he was jerked from his perch and thrown to the ground, tumbling over and over beneath a forest of arms and legs and sticks.

'Sorry,' gasped the player who had dislodged him. 'Hold still now and I'll have you up again.' Elbowing off the pack, he grabbed Hugh by the shirt front and hauled him back to his feet. As he did so Hugh felt something drop down inside his shirt – something cold and hard. 'There now,' said his unknown friend. 'You'll be right now,' and he winked and disappeared into the mêlée without a backward glance.

Hugh stumbled away, his arms wrapped across his chest. He could feel something like a small iron bar sitting on top of his belt, beneath his clothes. His head was reeling. It had all happened so quickly. Even Art, who had been leaning over the wall beside him, appeared to have seen nothing. But he knew what had been given him. He drew his cloak around it and kept his head down, terrified his face might betray his excitement. Not till he was back in the safety of their room did he dare to draw his treasure from his shirt.

'A file!' spluttered Art. 'Mother of God, a file! Will you look at it.'

'Where in the devil's name did you get it from?' demanded Henry.

They both began to fire questions at him, but he was too busy to answer them. Speed was essential now – in less than two hours they would be taken down to the refectory and then to their cell for the night. Sitting on the floor he began to work frantically on his fetters.

It seemed to take forever, but at last both his legs were free. Tossing the file to Henry he dragged the linen rope out of its chest and carried it into the privy. There was a small, barred window almost directly above the shaft and he tied the end of the rope to one of the bars. He returned to the others in time to see the older mac Shane pulling off his shackles. 'Here,' said Henry, standing up and passing the file to his brother, 'and hurry up, for Christ's sake – we haven't time to wait for you.'

Art's hands were clumsy. The harder he tried, the less progress he seemed to make. 'Let me do it for you,' said Hugh. He knelt beside his friend and began to saw at the iron. It yielded slowly, but eventually he had one ankle free and then the other. 'Done!' he said triumphantly. 'Now, let's be off.'

They ran into the privy. Henry was nowhere to be seen. 'Selfish pig,' said Art disgustedly. 'Could he not even wait for us?'

It was the first time Hugh had heard him criticise his brother. He grinned. 'Ah well,' he said, 'somebody had to test the rope.' He looked at Art. 'Will you go next?'

Art shook his head. Hugh knew he was thinking about Henry's taunts. He wanted to reassure him, but there was no time to argue. Swinging his legs over the edge of the privy shaft, he looked for the last time round his prison. He had expected to feel elation, but all that came to him was heaviness – a terrible and overwhelming sense of waste.

He had been a child when they brought him here – and now he was a man. Four years they had stolen from his life – four years of love and laughter and education – of hunting on Fanad peninsula with the MacSweeneys, of cattle raiding into Breifne with Eoghan mac Toole. Well, he would learn to laugh again. He would hunt, and fight, and somehow get the schooling of which they had cheated him. But nothing would ever bring back those four lost years. There was a great, black hole, somewhere in his being, and all the possibilities of the future would never fill it.

He looked at Art mac Shane. 'I'll make them pay,' he said. 'One day I'll make them pay.' And he lowered himself into the murky shaft.

thirteen

THE WIND PROWLED like a hungry wolf through the Wicklow Mountains, chasing the snow into frenzied squalls and snapping at the ears and fingers of the weary fugitives. They had been travelling for almost twenty-four hours now and Hugh was on the edge of exhaustion.

How could everything have gone so wrong? When he had crawled out of that stinking privy shaft onto the bank of the moat, freedom had seemed no more than an hour or so away, but since then there had been one disaster after another. First Art had injured his leg climbing down the privy. Then the promised horses had not arrived – taken from the stable at the last minute by somebody else – and finally at the foot of the castle wall, Henry mac Shane had deserted them.

'What signs of a fool do you see on me,' he had sneered, 'to be trusting the likes of Fiach mac Hugh O'Byrne – and him an ally of Hugh mac Ferdoragh? I'd as soon trust the devil. I'll find my own way home.' And, turning his back on his companions and the guide sent by

Fiach to escort them to Glenmalure, he had gone off into the night, leaving them to fend for themselves.

On foot, with no food for the journey, and without their cloaks – which they had been obliged to discard before squeezing down the privy – Hugh and Art had set off with their guide for Glenmalure. The trek had quickly turned into a nightmare. Even the weather seemed to conspire against them. Art had collapsed hours ago and they had been carrying him ever since. Now Hugh was wondering how much longer he could keep going himself. His clothes had started to freeze on his body. His hands were crippled, twisted into feeble claws by the icy wind; his feet felt like solid lumps of clay. He had no idea where they were or how far they had come and could only stumble forward, with Art a dead weight on his shoulder, trusting blindly to the knowledge and stamina of Fiach's guide.

At last, with the light fading, the young man called a halt. Hugh almost sobbed with relief as they lowered Art to the ground. Art groaned, and lay for a moment without moving before raising himself awkwardly on one elbow. 'Where are we?' he mumbled.

'We're after stopping for a bit of a rest,' Hugh told him.

Art eyed him anxiously. 'I'm too heavy for you. How far have we to go? – I'll wear you out.' His eyelids fluttered and he flopped back to the ground, as if the short speech had exhausted him.

Hugh's stomach knotted. 'Don't talk like a fool, man. Why, we are no more than a cock's crow from Glenmalure

– and Fiach mac Hugh waiting there to feast us like kings, with food and whiskey and the finest feather bed you ever slept in.' He looked to their guide, hoping for confirmation, but the young man said nothing.

Art gazed at both of them. 'It's a poor liar you are, Hugh Roe O'Donnell. Look at yourself – corpse-white and staggering like a poisoned dog. Another hour of this and we'll both be ravens' meat.' He jerked his chin at their guide. 'Tell him, lad.'

The young man hesitated. 'He has the truth of it,' he admitted at last. 'Glenmalure is just below us, but it's a rocky road down the mountainside and then the full of the glen to walk to Ballinacor. The way it is, you'll be lucky to make it yourself, unaided.'

'But we can't just leave him here.' A terrible suspicion wormed its way into Hugh's mind. He knew it was unworthy – was it himself to be poisoned by Henry mac Shane's cynicism? – but it would not go away. 'We can't abandon him,' he protested.

'Did I say we would? Look, there's a bit of a cave over there, under the ridge. Help me get him in there, out of the weather and then we'll decide what's to be done.'

Between them, they hoisted Art to his feet and half dragged, half carried him to the ridge. It was a walk of no more than a hundred paces, but it left Hugh gasping and staggering. As he finally ducked his head beneath the overhang, his legs buckled and he pitched forward, dragging the others down with him. His head hit the ground. He heard Art cry out, but the sound seemed to come from a long way away. It was some time before he became aware of his surroundings again.

The guide was hovering over him. 'Hugh! Hugh Roe – can you hear me? Are you hurt? Are you able to walk?'

Hugh wasn't sure. He dragged himself into a sitting position, but his head throbbed and the effort left him breathless. He thought about standing up – about walking – but even as his mind rehearsed the motions, he knew they were beyond him. 'I'm done in,' he confessed. 'I haven't it in me to take another step.'

Now it was the guide's turn to panic. 'You must' he insisted. 'I'll help you, we'll rest along the way, I'll carry you if I have to. Didn't I promise Fiach mac Hugh I'd bring you safe to Ballinacor? What will I tell him and I returning without you?'

'The truth,' said Hugh wearily. 'That we could go no further and sent you to fetch help.'

'But –'

'Someone has to go – we'll all be dead and we lying here much longer – and alone you'll have a better chance.'

'Ah, I don't know . . .' It clearly went against all the young man's training to leave them, but Hugh had the truth of it and in the end he had to give in. With many promises and anxious backward glances, he set off on his own for Ballinacor.

Night fell and a vast, cold emptiness settled over the mountain. The fugitives huddled together for warmth. At first they talked a little – trying to keep each other's spirits up – but soon Art fell asleep. Hugh was left to face the night alone. The dark hours passed slowly. The wind shifted and reached with icy fingers into the little cave – in reality, no more than a shallow recess beneath the rock-shelf. Hugh wrapped his arms round his aching body and thought longingly of his thick, warm mantle, back in the Bermingham Tower. Despite all his efforts, his mind kept returning to his abortive flight of twelve months ago. It is all happening again, he thought despondently.

By now the whole garrison would be out hunting him. He could imagine the hue and cry; and, as his ears strained for any tell-tale noises on the wind, he realised there was one terrible difference between this time and the last. When Hugh O'Toole had left him in the mountains twelve months ago, he had been torn between the fear of capture and the fear of death. This time it was only dis-covery he dreaded. Death held no terror – already his body felt like a dead thing. But capture . . .! If they did not hang him and put his head up on a spike, they would throw him back into that stone coffin beneath Dublin Castle – and this time it would be forever.

Gradually, the sky lightened and Hugh realised that it must be day. A day no better than the last – the wind was still howling like a stepmother's curse and driving gusts of snow into his pitiful little shelter. Art had not stirred. Hugh wondered should he wake him – he knew that men who fell asleep in snow often failed to wake at all – but his companion looked so peaceful, so blissfully unaware of his surroundings; it seemed too cruel to drag him back to reality. He pressed himself closer to Art's body, hoping the contact might somehow impart a flicker of warmth to both of them, and continued to wait.

Soon he began to feel drowsy himself. The pain of coldness had faded, leaving his body like a dead weight — something that no longer belonged to him. The snow, the wind, the hard, rocky ground — they all seemed unreal and very far away. Dimly he remembered he was supposed to stay awake, but he couldn't recall why. What did it matter? It was so much easier to let go. To lie here beside Art, to close his eyes and give himself to the darkness. To drift, to float, to let it run over him and carry him away . . .

● ● ●

He is drowning in Lough Swilly. The dark bubbling waters close above his head and thick weeds tangle his feet and draw him downward. He sinks unresisting — how peaceful it is to die. But he is cheating. It is not supposed to end like this. He has obligations. But what are they? — he tries to remember them, but they float somewhere in the back of his mind and he cannot hold on to them.

Figures move round him in the water — pale, naked figures. Voices whisper to him.

'We died for you, Red Hugh, son of O'Donnell. Will you leave us unavenged?'

'When Hugh succeeds Hugh . . . the last Hugh shall be Árd Rí of all Ireland and drive all the foreigners out.'

'You were not born to die in an English prison.'

What do they want of him? They cling like cobwebs and he tries to shake them off. Ghostlike they fade. But then comes another voice – one he has never heard before. 'Where are the champions of Ulster?' it demands, echoing a question he once asked himself, on a night so long ago in Rathmullen Castle. 'Where are the champions of Ulster? Has the hero-light died in the heart of Ireland?'

The reproach strikes to the very core of his being. Shamed, he kicks out, snapping the weed-fronds about his ankles, and thrusts himself up through the icy water. His head breaks the surface. He draws in the full of his lungs of air. The wind lifts him. Then, all at once, the waters have become a field of grass, a meadow strewn with white flowers, and he lying on it. A stranger is looking down at him – a tall figure wrapped in a long, green cloak.

The stranger's face is shadowed by his hood. He smiles – Hugh can feel the smile, even though he cannot see it. The man's hands move to unclasp a great, silver brooch at his throat. Fine, long-fingered hands they are, with skin translucent and pale as watered milk, and the bones seem to float in them like fronds of seaweed. Hugh stares, troubled by something that is not quite memory. I should know this man, he thinks, though he is sure he has never set eyes on him before.

With a fluid motion, the stranger sweeps off his cloak and tosses it, outspread, towards Hugh. It floats downwards, covering his world in a mantle of warm, green darkness.

'Sleep, son of O'Donnell. Sleep and live.'

It is the voice that called him from the waters – a gentle voice, but one of unchallengable authority. Hugh sighs and surrenders trustingly to its command.

❋ ❋ ❋

'You're wasting your time, man. He's frozen – stiff as an icicle.'

'And I tell you he's still breathing. Here, try this and see will it rouse him.'

The voices drifted down to Hugh out of a fog. Hands touched his face. Something wet trickled into his mouth. His mind stirred to life. Ale, it registered. Drink, swallow. But his body had forgotten how to obey.

'You see,' said the first voice. 'It runs straight out again.'

'Keep trying.' Another set of hands fumbled at Hugh's shoulders, shook him, gently at first, then with growing urgency. 'Hugh, Hugh Roe, open your eyes. We have you safe, you can't die on us now.'

Die? What on earth were they talking about? Of course he could not die. The stranger had laid a *geas* on him. 'Live,' he had said. But Hugh needed sleep. Could they not see that? Didn't they understand? 'Leave me be,' he tried to tell them, but as he moved his jaw, a trickle of ale ran down the back of his throat and he had to swallow. He choked and spluttered and was forced to gulp twice more, then his eyes opened and he saw he was lying on the mountainside again. The snow was blowing in his face, and his head was cradled on someone's arm. A ring of faces was looking down at him.

He blinked in bewilderment.

'Christ and all his saints,' cried one of the onlookers. 'He's alive!'

'What did I tell you?' said the man holding him. 'Sure, it's more than a bit of a blizzard it would take to finish off an O'Donnell. They breed them as tough as old bullocks up there in Tír Chonaill.'

'My sorrow that the other had not his stamina.'

The other! Memory came back to Hugh in a rush. 'Art?' he croaked. 'Art!' He struggled weakly in the arms of his rescuer.

'Easy, lad, easy,' said the man. 'I'm sorry. We are after doing everything we could for your friend, but . . .'

'Art? Where is he? I want to see him.'

The man pointed and Hugh rolled his head to look. Art lay on his back in the snow, calm and remote as a marble statue. His face stared up into the sky.

'Art! Ah, Jesu! Art, wake up!' Hugh flung himself out of the cradling arms and tried to crawl to his friend, but he hadn't the strength. His arms gave way. He collapsed in the snow, scrabbling uselessly with outstretched hands. 'You killed him,' he babbled, hardly knowing what he said. 'You killed him! Henry mac Shane was right. Why did we ever trust you?'

Hands lifted him, bore him away, wrapped him in a cloak to stop him struggling. 'Will you get that corpse out of sight,' a voice ordered sharply. 'Can't you see it upsets the lad?'

Two men lifted Art's frozen body and carried it away. Hugh watched them. They did it decently enough, but he could tell there was no real sorrow in them. He opened his mouth to yell at them again but his strength had gone. His rage crumpled into grief and he began to cry – a flood of silent tears that poured down his face, scalding his frost-bitten cheeks.

☙ ☙ ☙

Of the journey down the mountainside, he remembered almost nothing – hands, voices, the swaying motion of the men who carried him, and a dim knowledge of being passed from one shoulder to another like a sack of meal. Then, inexplicably, there was a roof over him; more hands; food and drink; voices again and finally sleep.

When he woke it was to the pain of frostbite – a pain like nothing he had ever known. It ran through his veins like rivers of fire, crippled him, stripped him of every last shred of dignity and left him threshing on his bed, raving and babbling like a woman in labour. 'Help me! Put an end to it! Ah, *Chreesta*, make it stop!' He heard the scream-ing voice, and knew it for his own, but was powerless to control it.

Hands reached out to him again. Pressed the rim of a cup against his mouth. 'Drink,' ordered a voice and a trickle of fiery liquid ran down his throat. He spluttered, tried to twist his head away, but the hands and voice were insistent. 'Drink, it will ease you.' There was no refusing. He swallowed – and swallowed again. His head swam, his mind wandered, the roof seemed to float up to the stars, and the pain dissolved into a red mist that faded into blackness.

● ● ●

The fire had gone, but a hundred smiths were at work inside his head, beating out horseshoes on his brain. His mouth felt like the inside of a bird's nest. He opened his eyes, groaned, and shut them again quickly. I'm drunk, he thought in astonishment. How did I ever get this way? Painfully, between hammer blows, he began to dredge up memories – fragments that shape-changed and slipped sideways when he tried to fit them together. Snow, mountains, a journey of some kind. And fear. But what had he to be afraid of? Where was he? Who had brought him here? What on God's earth was after happening to him?

If only he didn't feel so ill. Cautiously he opened his eyes again. He was lying on what felt like a bed of rushes. He saw walls and a ceiling, but they wouldn't stay still. They bulged and billowed like sails in the wind, till his head reeled from watching them. Dear God, he vowed, let me get well and I'll never drink again as long as I live. Suddenly his throat muscles went into spasm. The ground lurched beneath him, the walls rushed in on top of him, he rolled over and vomited on the floor.

Instantly there were people round him – holding him, wiping his face, offering sips of cold, clear water. 'There,' said a woman's voice. 'There now, it's all right. It's over. We have you safe, Hugh Roe.'

But it wasn't all right. It couldn't be. The voice was Róis O'Toole's. He was back in Castlekevin, trapped again by the swollen river, and Carew and his men coming any minute to seize him and drag him back to Dublin. 'Róis!' he screamed, clawing upward, clutching at her dress with crippled hands. 'Help me, Róis, for the love of God! Don't let them take me back.'

'Hush,' she said, 'hush, you are safe.' But he would not listen to her.

Then another face leaned down to him – a man's face. Strong hands closed over his own. A voice spoke from behind a tangle of black beard. 'Son, you are safe. You are in Ballinacor and I am Fiach mac Hugh O'Byrne. The devil himself wouldn't take you out of here and I not giving him leave.'

Ballinacor! Fiach mac Hugh. Hugh's battered mind repeated the words silently, over and over, like a prayer, till their meaning finally sank in. It was over. He was safe – safe from the meathook clutches of the English queen and the grim, grey battlements of Dublin Castle; safe from chains and leg irons; from Fitzwilliam's interrogation chamber, from that hell-hole in the bowels of the castle. He had escaped!

He wanted to shout, to fling his arms around Fiach and weep with gratitude, but he had no strength in him. He fell back on his pillow. Fiach's features wavered and dissolved before his eyes. With a garbled croak Hugh Roe slid into unconsciousness.

fourteen

SNUG IN HIS cocoon of safety and too weak to worry about the future, Hugh lay for a week in the little hut to which they had brought him. Róis stayed by his side day and night. She fed him, cleaned him, massaged his stiff and aching limbs and was there whenever the nightmares came, driving them off and soothing him back to sleep again. Sometimes Hugh wondered if she herself ever slept.

The nightmares were mostly of Art O'Neill. Hugh would be carrying him through the snow, his legs failing, his arms growing weaker from the cold. He would feel Art slip from his grasp, watch helplessly as the man slid towards a deep crevasse, and wake with a howl of anguish as Art plunged over the edge into blackness. Or he would be standing over Art's body, defending it from a pack of hungry wolves that circled, watching and waiting their moment to slip under his guard and seize their prey.

He knew what triggered the nightmares. They were the questions he was afraid to ask. What had really happened up there on the mountainside? Not murder – he would never let himself believe that – and yet . . . You could let a man die – and him so far gone with the cold – without actually killing him. What had really happened to Art mac Shane O'Neill?

He must put it behind him. Art was gone. Nothing could bring him back again and the truth was something he would never know for certain. Perhaps that was better so. But that dead body and impassive, white-marble face would remain with him for the rest of his life – another ghost in his spectral following.

To stop himself from brooding, he began to concentrate on his own troubles. He had frostbite. As his strength returned, it bothered him more and more. His body was losing its stiffness, his hands were slowly and painfully returning to normal, but his feet had no feeling in them at all. Black, swollen and useless, they protruded from his ankles like two great lumps of black pudding. The sight of them horrified him, even though Róis assured him they were not as bad as they looked and that all would be well and he only having patience.

He pretended to believe her, but patience was a luxury he knew he could not afford. Despite Fiach's boasts, Glenmalure was not a safe haven. By now, Fitzwilliam must know where he was, and if the Lord Deputy did not dare to enter the glen in force, it could always be done by stealth. It would take only one man with a knife – and a dead hostage was less troublesome than an escaped one. Besides, he could not stay here forever. Fitzwilliam's troopers had only to sit outside, like cats round a mouse hole, waiting for him to make his move.

It seemed ungenerous to discuss these fears with Fiach and Róis, so he brooded on them privately, and it was while he was sunk in gloom one evening that Fiach brought a visitor to him. Hugh recognised the young man immediately – Turlough Buí O'Hagan, Hugh mac Ferdoragh's message bearer – his eyes, ears and mouthpiece wherever cunning and discretion were necessary. The English had a word for such men; 'pursuivants', they called them – something less than a herald yet not quite a spy. And Turlough O'Hagan was a prince among pursuivants.

Turlough it was who had brought letters and messages from his lord to the hostages in Dublin Castle and, in the case of information not fitted for English scrutiny, procured trustworthy servants to smuggle it into the prisons. Turlough knew everything about everybody, and could judge to the last whisper how much to tell – and to whom. Hugh's heart leapt at the sight of him – if there was one man who could bring him safe to Tír Chonaill, that man was Turlough Buí O'Hagan.

O'Hagan seemed equally delighted at their meeting. 'Doesn't it do my heart good to see you, Hugh Roe O'Donnell,' he declared, 'and you out of that stinking prison and your own man again. Fiach is after telling me the time you had of it, out there in the mountains.'

Hugh shuddered. 'It was no banquet,' he agreed. 'Are . . . are you come to bring me home?'

'I am, lad – and beacons burning on every hilltop from Innishowen to the Erne to welcome you.'

Hugh closed his eyes and a thousand pictures danced behind them. He felt tears of sheer happiness welling up inside him. Then he remembered. 'But . . . the frostbite.' He twitched up the blanket so Turlough could see for himself. 'I can't walk.'

The young man laughed. 'Sure and haven't they horses enough in Glenmalure to do the walking for you, and I with money in my purse to buy the best of them?'

'But I mean literally, Turlough – not a step – I can't even stand.'

'And why would you be needing to? Haven't I arms to lift you in and out of the saddle – even carry you and it necessary?'

He made it sound so easy – a journey from one side of the country to the other, hunted like hares all the way, and he was treating it like a jaunt from Beleek to Ballyshannon. His self-possession and easy confidence inspired trust and Hugh felt a load slip from his shoulders. For four years he had waged a lonely struggle – dependent entirely on his own courage. Now Turlough would weigh the risks, make the decisions, take on the responsibility. The relief was intoxicating.

Turlough seemed to read his mind. 'We are proud of you, Hugh Roe,' he said softly. 'You are after bearing your troubles like a champion. Now they are over. Trust me – I'll see you safely home.'

They started out the next day, accompanied by an escort of Fiach's best men who would see them as far as the Liffey. The English were reported to be watching all the fords, but Fiach knew of a spot, perilously close to Dublin, where, he said, a crossing might be made by anyone bold or desperate enough to attempt it.

'It will mean going back almost to Dublin though,' he warned, 'and passing right under the walls of Dundrum Castle.'

Turlough frowned. 'You are sure there is no safer route – through the mountains?'

'Not on horseback.'

They both looked at Hugh and he, looking down at his feet, cursed himself again for a useless cripple. Turlough laughed. 'Then through Dundrum it shall be, and, sure, isn't that the very last place they'll be looking for us?'

Hugh could only pray he was right. They passed Dundrum Castle just before sunset. It was an experience he hoped he would never have to repeat. In the shadow of the walls, his stomach knotted and his heart thumped like a drum. Surely anyone looking down from those walls must recognise him. But no one challenged them. It was like a miracle.

Once clear of the castle they turned north-west and continued on until they reached the Liffey. Hugh stared, dismayed, into the swirling water. Was this the ford?

Winter rains had turned it into a raging torrent. They couldn't possibly cross here. Even Turlough seemed taken aback, but Walter Reagh FitzGerald, Fiach's son-in-law, led them confidently upstream and at last they came to a bend where silt had formed a little spit on either bank and created a crossing of sorts.

In summer it would have afforded easy enough passage but now, with the river in full flood, it looked anything but safe. Turlough and Walter Reagh dismounted and walked out onto the sand-spit to survey their options. Hugh watched them talking. After a long discussion they returned to the group.

'We'll cross four abreast – as tightly bunched as possible,' Turlough told them. 'And Hugh Roe will ride in the middle.'

Hugh didn't argue. The horses were nervous and took a lot of coaxing, but once in the river they proved sure-footed enough. Wedged in the middle of a solid block of riders, Hugh crossed without mishap. The water was deep though, and bitterly cold. It lapped around the flanks of his horse, soaking him almost to the thighs. He couldn't help wondering what further damage it was doing to his feet. As he emerged on the far bank, the wind pierced his wet clothes like needles. His teeth began to chatter.

Turlough, who had crossed at the front of the column, was waiting for him. He lifted the boy from his horse and without ceremony stripped him of his sodden trousers and put him into a dry pair. Then he dried Hugh's feet, swathed them in fresh bandages and slipped over them the clumsy leather bags Róis had fashioned to serve him as shoes.

'Right,' he said, as soon as this was finished. 'Let's be having you back on your horse now. The sooner we are away the better.'

He hoisted Hugh into the saddle and they were about to ride off when they heard a commotion on the far bank. Hugh looked back in alarm. Walter Reagh and his men, having bid them farewell, had returned across the river – the last riders were just emerging from the water on the other side. The shouts, however, came, not from them but from another man – a stranger – who was spurring up the path towards the group. The man was hollering in English – demanding to know who they were and where they were bound.

Walter Reagh waited till all his men were back on dry land, then edged his mount a few paces towards the Englishman. The man reined in and watched him suspiciously. 'Who are you?' he demanded again, 'and what is your business here?'

'We are clansmen of Fiach mac Hugh O'Byrne,' said Walter Reagh, 'and our business is no man's but our own. What do you want with us?'

'I have orders from the Lord Deputy to question all travellers. We are seeking the prisoner, Hugh Roe O'Donnell, lately escaped from Dublin Castle.'

'Prisoner is it?' Walter Reagh laughed shortly. 'Well you'll find no prisoners here.' And he let fly with a string of obscenities that would have singed the man's ears had he understood Irish – which Hugh doubted. There could be no mistaking the meaning of the words though. Hugh saw the man's hand drop to his sword-hilt. Walter Reagh laughed contemptuously. He waved an arm to his followers and the whole troop swept past the Englishman and away into the gathering darkness. As they disappeared into the night, Walter Reagh's voice floated back across the water. 'O'Donnell *abú*!' he shouted. 'God's blessing on your journey. Remember me to Hugh mac Ferdoragh.'

It was a reckless gesture, for the Saxon, recognising the names and sensing the words were not directed at him, glanced for the first time across the river – straight at Hugh and Turlough. Turlough didn't wait to see what would happen next. 'Ride,' he yelled at Hugh. 'Ride for your life,' and Hugh didn't need telling twice. He dug his knees into his horse's sides and the grey flew down the narrow track with Turlough's mount hard on its heels.

Not till they had put several miles between themselves and the river did Turlough call on him to ease his pace. He slowed to a jog and his guide moved up beside him. 'Is he following us?' asked Hugh.

Turlough Buí shook his head. 'He'd be the fool. No man in his right mind would cross that river in the dark and he on his own. But he'll be away to Dublin as fast as he can ride with news of what he saw.' He swore softly. 'The devil mend Walter Reagh and his big mouth. There'll be no sleep for us tonight now. I'll not rest easy till I have you safe across the Boyne.'

They rode for what seemed hours, pushing their horses as hard as they dared. Hugh had no idea where they were going. It was north, and that was good enough for him. For a while the thought of home and the sheer joy of riding unfettered for the first time in four years was enough to keep him going. But it couldn't last. He was unused to exercise and still weak from his ordeal in the mountains. Long before morning he was falling asleep in the saddle, riding purely by instinct and relying on Turlough to make sure he didn't fall off.

At last Turlough called a halt. Hugh lifted his head and saw water in front of him. A river . . . but surely they had already crossed the river. Why had they gone back again? He tried to ask Turlough, but he was so tired even his voice wouldn't work. The words slid out sideways and he sounded like The O'Neill after a drinking binge. Fortunately his guide seemed to understand him.

'It's all right, lad,' he chuckled. 'We're after reaching the Boyne. Soon you'll be able to rest.'

Rest! He swayed in the saddle and dreamed about it. But if this was the Boyne . . . 'A town,' he faltered, 'should there not be a town here?' and he tried to dredge the name out of his memory.

'Drogheda,' agreed Turlough. 'But we are not going through the town. They may have the bridge watched.'

Drogheda . . . through the town . . . Snatches of memory flickered past him. He giggled light-headedly. 'Eoghan,' he mumbled. 'Eoghan O'Gallagher – like the pox through an English castle.'

'What?' Turlough rode closer and peered into his exhausted features. 'God help us, Hugh Roe, you have the face of a man at his own funeral. Here, give me your reins and let you hold on to the saddle. It's not much farther now.'

Obediently, Hugh passed them over. It was easier to let Turlough lead him. He closed his eyes and when he next opened them he found they had stopped again. He could see a small dwelling on the bank of the river and a fisherman's curragh pulled up on a strip of sand at the water's edge. Beside it stood Turlough, deep in conversation with the man who, presumably, was its owner. As Hugh watched, the two men shook hands. Turlough came back to the horses.

'I'm after striking a bargain,' he said. 'Your man there will row us across the river, then bring the horses through the town for us.'

Hugh looked at the fisherman, who was already dragging his boat into the water. Can we trust him? he wondered. He looked harmless enough – stooped and careworn, with the shuffling gait of the very old – but looks could be deceptive and the heavy cloak that wrapped him from top to toe could have disguised almost anything. Suppose he was not really a fisherman at all? Suppose he was an agent of Fitzwilliam's sent to trap them?

But Turlough trusted him. And this man had a boat. It was all too complicated and anyway, Hugh was too tired to argue. He slid from the saddle into Turlough's arms, and once in the curragh, promptly fell asleep.

He woke as Turlough was carrying him up the bank on the other side. 'There now,' said his guide, settling him beneath the skeleton of a hawthorn tree. 'Let you rest here a moment. I want a quick word with your man here before he goes back for the horses.'

Hugh watched him walk down to the water's edge. He was too far away to hear what passed between the two men, but he saw Turlough put something into the other's hand and watched the fisherman pull out into the stream and begin to row back across the river. He shivered. Was he imagining it or was there was something sinister about that shrouded figure?

Turlough came back up the bank. 'Well, he has one half of what I promised him. Please God, he'll come back for the other.'

He smiled, but Hugh was sure he was more anxious than he let on. He wanted to ask him how he had found the man – how he knew they could trust him – but he held his tongue. Turlough had promised to bring him safely home – he had to believe in him.

It wasn't easy though. As the hours crept by with no sign of the fisherman, doubts tormented him. What if the man did not return? What if he was stopped and questioned at the bridge? And what if he was in the pay of the English? Hugh was convinced he had seen the old man before – and where could that ever have been but in Dublin Castle? Perhaps, even now, he was leading Fitzwilliam's soldiers to their hiding place.

Hugh glanced at his companion. Turlough was pacing up and down the river bank. It is all going wrong, thought Hugh. It is Castlekevin all over again. Fear, colder than the waters of the Liffey, washed over his body. This time they would surely hang him. But before they did, they would want to know who had aided him. They would drag him back to that room beneath the castle and then . . . Oh *Chreesta*! He pressed both hands to his mouth to choke back a sob of terror.

Turlough hurried back to him. 'Ah, come on, lad. Have faith. Your man won't let us down.' He lifted his head to gaze at something behind Hugh's shoulder and his face creased into a smile. 'Look,' he said softly. 'Didn't I tell you?'

Hugh turned. There, coming out of the shadows towards them was the muffled figure – alone – riding one horse and leading the other. Hugh choked back a cry of relief. Turlough ran forward to greet their champion. The old fisherman dismounted. Hugh heard the murmur of voices, saw a purse change hands. He watched Turlough take the reins of the horses and begin to lead them back. The old man hunched his shoulders against the wind and started back the way he had come. How frail he looked, thought Hugh, with a sudden stab of guilt. How long and cold his journey would be on foot, back through the town to that little hut on the other bank. He felt ashamed of his unfounded suspicions and hoped Turlough had been generous. He cupped his hands to his mouth. 'God keep you safe,' he called.

The man stopped. He turned, his back straightened. The years seemed to drop away from him. His whole figure was suddenly imbued with strength and vitality. He lifted his head, still hidden in the hood of his mantle and looked directly at Hugh. 'A blessing on your journey, son of O'Donnell,' he said and he raised his hand in benediction.

Hugh gasped. He knew that voice! And then he noticed something else. The stranger's cloak, that had seemed grey in the darkness, was grass green in the dawning light, and the raised hand was pale and translucent, with bones that moved in it like fronds of seaweed.

FIFTEEN

TURLOUGH CAME UP with the horses. He was smiling broadly. 'So, are you fit to ride again? We are no more than a few miles from Mellifont now, and there you will be able to rest.'

Hugh nodded. Turlough lifted him back into the saddle and, mounting his own horse, gathered both sets of reins into his own hands. Hugh made no protest. His mind was still in a daze. '*A blessing on your journey*,' the stranger had said. Not 'God's blessing,' but '*a* blessing' – as though he had some power in himself to bestow it. What manner of man could do that? An angel, maybe – a guardian angel sent from heaven to protect him? Such a miracle was not beyond thinking of, but surely even an angel could only bestow blessings in God's name?

And how was it that Turlough had noticed nothing unusual? Hugh shot a sideways glance at his companion – Turlough Buí O'Hagan, so competent, so down-to-earth, so . . . so unastonishable. Perhaps, he thought with shock, Turlough was not meant to know – just as he himself still did not know the stranger's name. They had met twice – in his dream on the mountain and now here at the Boyne – he had an odd feeling that they would meet again. One day it would all make sense, but for the moment it was enough that the stranger had given him back his courage.

He was convinced now that he would not be caught. The stranger had practically guaranteed it. Had he declared in so many words, 'You are under my protection,' he could not have made his promise more emphatic. As they continued their journey northward, Hugh's heart bubbled over with joy. Every step now was bringing him closer to home, and though the miles sometimes seemed endless, though his feet hurt abominably and his whole body often ached with exhaustion, nothing could destroy his confidence.

Even two days later when they reached Dundalk, and English patrols on all the lesser roads obliged them to pass right through the town itself, still he did not falter. He held his head high and sat his horse with an assurance that amazed his guide. 'My soul, Hugh Roe, it's the impudence of an outlaw you have,' Turlough chuckled, as they finally left the town behind. 'And in those English clothes, don't you look the very picture of some arrogant Saxon lordling.'

Hugh laughed and looked down at the outlandish garments given him by Sir Garrett Moore, in whose home – Mellifont Abbey – they had rested the previous night. Mellifont had been an astonishing experience. The young Englishman had treated them royally – and he with a father on the Privy Council. Hugh mac Ferdoragh's influence, it seemed, reached even into the heart of the English administration. Hugh had come away utterly confused. Perhaps all Englishmen were not irrevocably damned after all. Maybe, here and there, one or two of them had managed to escape the misfortune of their birth.

He turned and glanced back at the town. Once, long ago, Dundalk had been Cuchulainn's stronghold. Now it marked the boundary of the English Pale. They had passed through it into Hugh mac Ferdoragh's country and every mile from now on would bring them deeper under his protection. Defiantly, Hugh snatched off his hat, and shook free his hair to stream like a bright red banner in the wind. '*Lámh Dearg abú*!' he yelled: Cheers for the Red Hand – the war cry of the O'Neills.

Turlough grinned at him. They both knew it was not for Turlough Luineach that he cheered.

Hugh had looked forward to a hero's welcome from Hugh mac Ferdoragh. It was a great disappointment when Turlough led him cautiously through the gates of Dungannon Castle and whisked him off to a secluded apartment well away from the main hall. He was tired of skulking and hiding – he had escaped and he wanted to celebrate his triumph. Turlough only smiled at his complaints. 'Sure, it's not by taking foolish risks your man here is after living so long with one foot in each camp,' he said. 'Didn't Fitzwilliam write to him – and you not two days out of prison –

demanding his help to recapture you. Is he the fool to be flaunting your presence under his very roof?'

Hugh sighed and didn't answer. He could appreciate Hugh mac Ferdoragh's caution, but that didn't mean he had to like it.

He didn't have to wait long, though, before receiving a visit from his champion. Hardly had Turlough settled him in his new quarters, when the door opened and the man himself stood in the doorway. Hugh looked at him, suddenly shy and tongue-tied. He owed everything to this man – his freedom, possibly even his life. How could he begin to thank him.

His host grinned at him. 'Well, Hugh Roe, am I after keeping my word?'

'You are. My soul, but you are.'

'And Turlough is after taking good care of you?'

Hugh turned to look at the man who had smuggled him halfway across Ireland, under the very noses of his jailers. For the first time he noticed how tired Turlough looked, and realised with a twinge of guilt that his guide had probably barely slept in the last few days. Turlough had been like a rock. He had never chided, never complained, never once shown the least sign of anxiety, yet there must have been times when he had feared for both their lives. Hugh reached out to grasp his friend's hand. 'Turlough Buí O'Hagan,' he said, 'is a man to make Finn mac Cumhaill look small. There is nothing I could ever give him that would be payment enough for what he is after doing for me.'

Hugh mac Ferdoragh nodded. The gleam in his eye told what value he put on those words – and on the man who had earned them. 'And a champion needs his food,' he declared. 'Away to your supper, Turlough, and a good night's rest. Tomorrow I will thank you properly.'

Soon after Turlough had left, two servants came in bringing food for Hugh. If the Lord of Dungannon was obliged to keep his guest hidden, he clearly had no intention of keeping him unfeasted. There were lashings and leavings and Hugh did justice to everything. His host did not eat, but shared a flask of wine before departing to his own supper. 'They'll miss me in the hall and I not there to eat with them,' he explained. 'Have you everything you need?'

'I have,' said Hugh.

His host smiled. 'Then let you rest now. We'll talk further in the morning. In the meantime, I'll have someone come to bathe your feet, and change those bandages. And later I'll send a man to pass the night here. You can call on him and you needing anything.'

Hugh lay back on his pillows, soaking up the sheer luxury of rest. No more disguises and secret journeys; no more cold, silent rides through night-time forests. When he left here, it would be under the protection of Hugh mac Ferdoragh, and with a company of his host's own bodyguard for an escort.

He looked around the room. It brought back memories of another night in an Irish castle. Rathmullen – was it still as he remembered it? Were the little waves still restless on Lough Swilly, did the eagle hunt above the peninsula? Soon he would see for himself. Soon he would sit again in the banqueting hall with Donal Gorm MacSweeney and listen to the songs of the MacSweeney bards. He would watch snow fall over Bearnas Mór, return to his foster home at Castle Doe and hear mass again in the friary on Sheephaven Bay – Sweet Jesu, to smell incense again and hear the sound of plainchant! He closed his eyes and let the music follow him into his dreams.

The clunk of a door opening and closing brought him out of a deep sleep. He opened his eyes. A girl was standing by the bed looking down at him. She held a bowl and a jug of steaming water and at first he thought she must be a servant – but her clothes were not those of a kitchen maid and there was an air about her that said she was more used to giving orders than obeying them.

She set the jug and bowl down on the bedside table and smiled at him. He smiled back, foolishly. Her gaze embarrassed him – almost as though she were seeing him naked.

'So', she said, and her voice had a gently mocking ring. 'The great Hugh Roe O'Donnell honours us with his company. My father tells me your feet are in need of bathing.'

'Your father?' Hugh gaped. He felt the blood rush to his cheeks. 'Your father! Then you . . . I mean . . . You must be . . .?'

'I am Róis O'Neill.'

Holy Columcille! The girl he was supposed to be

married to! He tried to think of something intelligent to say, but his mind seemed to have shrivelled like a dried-up cowpat. 'I . . . ah . . .' he stumbled, 'I . . . um . . . that is . . . we're not after meeting, I'm thinking. Your father never brought you to Tír Chonaill.'

Her smile gave nothing away. 'My father has many daughters. It is not his way to be taking them on idle journeys.'

Why was she teasing him! Couldn't she see how awkward he felt? God alone knew, four years in an English prison was no way to acquire social graces. Was she angry with him? Did she think the so-called marriage had been his idea? He wanted to defend himself, but the words just would not come. He could only stare at her, knowing full well how ridiculous he must look.

'Are your feet bad?' she asked, still with that enigmatic smile on her face. 'Will I bathe them for you?'

'I . . . I'd like that. Thank you.'

She moved to the foot of the bed and began to unwrap his bandages. Suddenly, her expression changed. 'Holy Mother of God! What in the world are they after doing to you?'

'It's frostbite,' he explained. 'They look worse than they are.'

'Even so . . . Will I have our physician see to them?'

He shook his head. 'There's no need. They'll keep till I get home. MacDunleavy will know what to do for them.'

She made no reply to that, and he wondered if he had

offended her; but he could not tell her his real reason for declining her offer – that he was simply too afraid of what her physician might tell him.

Róis worked deftly and unhurriedly, sponging his swollen feet, drying them and re-bandaging them with clean linen. 'There, now,' she said at last, securing the last strip. 'Does that feel better?'

It did. 'Thank you,' he mumbled, wishing desperately he did not feel so clumsy.

She began to gather up the soiled linen and drop it into the bowl. *Say something*, urged his mind. For the love of God, speak to her now, before she goes. You may not get another chance. 'Róis,' he stammered. 'Róis, I . . . I'm sorry.'

'Sorry?' She straightened and regarded him with amused eyes. 'And what in the world have you to be sorry for, Hugh Roe O'Donnell?'

'For . . . ah, you know. Your father . . . and what he wrote to Walsingham . . . and . . .'

She looked at him thoughtfully for a moment, and then she laughed – a warm, merry sound. 'Let you not fear, Hugh Roe. I am my father's daughter, and no more to be commanded than he is. When I marry, I will choose my own time and my own partner.'

And with those words she picked up her bowl and jug and departed. Hugh lay on the bed and gazed at the door she had closed behind her. He felt more confused than ever. Had that been a reassurance or a rejection?

He stayed at Dungannon for four days and each morning Hugh mac Ferdoragh came to talk with him. The picture he drew of the state of affairs in Tír Chonaill was not comforting. 'The sad truth is,' he told Hugh, 'your father is no longer fit to hold the reins. He is senile. The Cenél Chonaill must have a new chieftain and every man within bowshot of the title is trying his strength to see will it be him.'

'But Hugh mac Hugh Dubh is the elected *tánaiste*. Why do they not choose him?'

His host looked at him sharply. 'Why do you think?'

He hesitated. 'My mother?'

'You have the truth of it. What power still remains with The O'Donnell, she exercises, and she will have no one but you. Two men she is after sending to their graves already, let you remember. But now your uncle, Hugh mac Hugh Dubh and your cousin, Niall Garbh, are both pressing their claims and the clans are split in their support.'

This was not the homecoming Hugh had dreamed about. He looked helplessly at his host. 'I never wanted this. I never asked to be chieftain. I would serve happily as *tánaiste* to Hugh mac Hugh Dubh.'

'I believe you. But neither he nor Niall Garbh is strong enough to unite Tír Chonaill now. The clans are tearing themselves apart and, in the meantime, the Englishman, Willis – and his men, holed up in Donegal Friary – rampage through the country from Lough Erne to Glen

Columcille, and no one is able – or willing – to prevent them.'

The words turned in Hugh's heart like a knife. He thought again of the desecrated friary – of its guardian, gentle Tadhg O'Boyle, murdered in his own cloister. 'I'll have them out,' he vowed. 'I'll raise an army and drive them back to where they came from.'

'You will not,' said his host sternly. 'Not until you are fully well again. Tomorrow I am sending you to the Maguire at Enniskillen. He will see you safely to Bally-shannon and there you will rest until your physician says you are fit for action. You'll be no use to anyone and you unable to walk.'

Hugh shut his mouth mutinously. Nothing is changed, he thought. Here I am, not two weeks out of prison and everyone giving me orders again. He was happy though, to be going to Enniskillen. Hugh Maguire was his cousin and a man he had idolised since childhood – a bold, laughing giant of a man, who lived life with an enthusiasm that bordered on recklessness. Great tales had filtered back to Dublin of the doings of Hugh Maguire. When the Lord Deputy had threatened to put a sheriff into Fermanagh, wasn't Maguire reputed to have told him: 'Send one, by all means, but be sure to let me know his blood price first, and I to levy it on the clans when they kill him.' Yes, it would be a joy to renew his friendship with Hugh Maguire.

Eager though he was to move on, he still found himself a little nervous when the day came for his departure.

Mounted in the midst of his escort, he cast a long, final glance round the courtyard of Dungannon Castle. He had felt safe here, but the future to which he was riding seemed suddenly very uncertain. He hoped his apprehension didn't show in his face.

Hugh mac Ferdoragh had come to see him off, so had Turlough – and so, somewhat to his embarrassment, had Róis. Turlough had once more been obliged to lift him into his saddle and it embarrassed him that Róis should have to see him so. She had not been back to his room since that first evening, and he still did not know how she felt about him.

He felt his face redden as she stepped forward to say goodbye.

'God speed the journey Hugh Roe,' she said solemnly, and then she smiled. 'They tell me you are to be the new O'Donnell.'

'It . . . it seems likely.'

'Well now,' she put her head on one side and looked at him. 'The Lady O'Donnell – sure and wouldn't that be a grand title.' Then, before he could answer, she laughed and added. 'But wouldn't your mother be having to surrender it first, I'm thinking.'

He could only gape at her, amazed at both her boldness and perception. She held out her hand and he took it and raised it to his lips. Then she turned and went back to her father. Hugh mac Ferdoragh raised his own hand. 'God's blessing on you, Hugh Roe. Remember me to the Maguire – and mind what I said now about resting.'

Hugh smiled and mumbled a pretended promise.

His host signalled to the leader of the escort and the company moved off through the gates. Hugh turned once to look back at the castle, but Róis had already gone inside.

❀ ❀ ❀

If Hugh mac Ferdoragh had found it necessary to entertain his guest in secret, the Maguire felt no such constraint. Enniskillen Castle threw open its doors to the escapee. Every man, woman and child of Maguire's household came down to the gates to welcome him. A skirl of pipes greeted him as he was borne in triumph to the banqueting hall, and if trumpeters could have been found to proclaim his coming from the battlements, then doubtless, thought Hugh with amusement, Maguire would have had them, too.

The hall was a blaze of light and colour. Torches flared, firelight glinted off the shields and weapons displayed around the walls, banners hung from every beam, and the air was pungent with the aroma of cooked meat and new-baked bread. Servants ran to and fro with jugs and platters and every table was piled high with food. Hugh felt light-headed. His mind reeled with the sheer extravagance of it all. His cousin plied him with food and drink. Hugh tried to answer all his questions, but the Maguire talked so fast and leapt so bewilderingly from one topic to another, it was difficult to keep up with him. His exuberance reminded Hugh of Eoghan O'Gallagher, who would be waiting to greet him tomorrow in Bally-shannon.

One more day and he would finally be home again – his heart quickened at the thought.

Around him, the chatter in the hall died to an ambient hum as everyone applied themselves to the serious business of eating. At last even the most prodigious appetites were sated. Noise levels rose again and eyes turned towards the high table. It was time for the entertainment. Hugh Maguire jumped to his feet. 'A health!' he shouted. 'A health to Hugh Roe O'Donnell, and he after laughing in the face of danger and coming safe to Enniskillen, despite every English soldier between here and Glenmalure.'

'Hugh Roe O'Donnell,' echoed the company.

Hugh felt a bit of an imposter. He wanted to protest that all he had done was follow orders: others had done the planning and taken most of the risks. But he needn't have worried, the Maguire was only warming to his theme. Over the next half-hour they drank to Hugh mac Ferdoragh and Turlough Buí, to Fiach mac Hugh, to Róis O'Toole, to Walter Reagh, to Garrett Moore; to everyone who had aided Hugh's flight in any way. They even drank to poor, dead Art mac Shane.

Finally, when everyone had run out of inspiration, the tables were cleared and the dancing started. Hugh shivered as two harps struck up the first air and the hall dissolved into a swirling mass of dancers. The music ran through his veins like blood. This was his heritage – his birthright – the life he had hungered for over four bitter years. This was what it meant to be Irish.

The musicians started with a gentle measure but gradually the tempo increased. Harps sang, pipes wailed, *bodhráns* thundered a compulsive beat. And dozens of feet stamped patterns on the floor. Faster and faster they trod and faster and faster played the musicians.

Hugh glanced at his cousin, sitting beside him. Hugh Maguire's eyes were shining, his fingers drummed a tattoo against his thigh. Suddenly, as if he could contain himself no longer, the Maguire sprang to his feet with a triumphant yell and leapt into the midst of the dancers.

The music quickened. The men circled their chieftain. Dance had become ritual, the display a contest. For a big man, Maguire was incredibly agile. He leapt, he turned, his feet drummed fiercely on the floor. It was as though the music had possessed him. One by one the other contestants dropped out, but still Maguire danced. His face shone, his brown curls flew wildly round his head, beads of sweat glistened on his forehead and spread in damp patches across the back of his shirt. Finally he had the floor to himself. The music rose in one burst of demonic fury – and collapsed in on itself with a mighty wail. Bereft of its support, Hugh Maguire collapsed also, laughing.

He sprawled on the floor, flat on his back with arms outspread, still laughing and gasping and shouting for a jar of ale to revive him, and the audience rose with a spontaneous roar.

Hugh Roe too leapt cheering to his feet. But pain knifed through them, dropping him back into his chair. He looked down at his feet. Soft and useless as a couple of sea-sponges – would he ever again leap into a ring of dancers and stamp his feet to the rhythm of a goatskin drum? Would he even walk again? He remembered something Hugh mac Ferdoragh had said: 'You'll be no use to anyone and you unable to walk.' It was brutally true. The law was absolute. If he could not walk he could not be The O'Donnell. No clan would elect a chieftain and he maimed.

sixceen

SMALL FISH SCALES of light danced across the surface of Lough Erne and the air was so clean it almost hurt Hugh's lungs. He sucked in a great breath and, from his seat in the prow of the boat, stared about him in amazement. How could he have lived so long in the midst of all this beauty and never noticed it? Did you have to be deprived of something before you could appreciate it?

The rowers dipped their oars and the boat sliced silently through the water. They were making for the mouth of the lough – the narrow neck where it became a river. He was almost home now – on the further shore an escort would be waiting to fetch him to Ballyshannon. He stared across the water with narrowed eyes and imagined he could see figures on the bank.

Another few moments and wishful thinking became reality. A large company of horsemen had come out of the trees and was drawn up along the shoreline. With each stroke of the oars, Hugh could make them out more clearly – their banners, their horses, the colour of their clothes. The man leading them wore a sky-blue mantle. He was tall and broad shouldered and his long, fair hair streamed in the wind each time he moved his head. Hugh recognised him immediately. His heart began to thump. He cupped his hands to his mouth. 'Eoghan!' he yelled. 'Eoghan O'Gallagher!'

Eoghan raised clasped hands above his head and shook them triumphantly. His voice drifted back across the water. 'O'Donnell *abú*! A hundred thousand welcomes!'

The entire company took up the cry and Maguire's oarsmen began to cheer as well. They quickened their stroke and the boat shot forward like a hunting otter. As they neared the shore, Eoghan leapt from his horse and waded out knee-deep into the freezing water to meet them. 'God bless the day,' he exclaimed, 'and I afraid I'd never see it. Is it really yourself, Hugh Roe?'

'It is,' laughed Hugh, 'unless they're after swapping me for some other man along the way, and forgetting to tell me about it.' He reached out a hand to his friend. 'Ah, *Chreesta*, it's good to see your ugly mug again, Eoghan.'

'And yours. And all Tír Chonaill rejoicing to have you home again.'

'All?' Hugh raised an eyebrow. 'That's not exactly how I heard it.'

'Well, as many as have any sense.' Eoghan grinned, but then became serious again. 'There's no use to talk, Hugh, the country's in a bad way. But discussion of that can wait. You're home, that's the important thing.' He hesitated. 'How is my father?'

'He's well,' said Hugh. 'Or as well as any man can be and he a prisoner.' A wave of anger swept over him. 'He was my father's right hand, Eoghan, the one man he could always rely on. I feel the want of him already.'

'All Tír Chonaill feels the want of him,' said Eoghan. He bit his lip and was silent for a moment. Then: 'Look,' he said, lifting his head and pointing skyward, 'an eagle. There was one hunting over the Fanad Peninsula that day. Remember?'

'I do,' said Hugh, following his gaze. He smiled. 'But I never expected you would.'

'How would I forget?' said Eoghan softly. 'Isn't every detail of that morning stamped on my mind like words in a book? Every cloud in the sky, every ripple on the water – why, I could number the pebbles on the shore and you asking me.'

Hugh grinned. 'And Donal saying you hadn't as much poetry in you as a bull's backside.' He prodded his friend in the ribs. 'He was wrong. You have!'

Eoghan roared with laughter. 'The devil mend you, Hugh Roe O'Donnell. You have a tongue on you sharp enough to cut a man's throat. Was that an insult or a compliment?'

❀ ❀ ❀

Ballyshannon honoured the return if its hero in a manner to rival even Maguire's hospitality. The feasting and dancing went on into the early hours of the morning and Hugh celebrated the fullness of his freedom on a wave of whiskey-winged euphoria. He woke the next morning with a sore head and an inevitable sense of deflation. MacDunleavy the physician came to examine his feet. He poked and prodded for a long time and Hugh watched him anxiously. 'Well,' he demanded at last, 'are they going to mend? Will I walk again?'

'I don't know.' said MacDunleavy honestly. 'It is still too early to tell. God willing they will heal, but only if you give them absolute rest.'

'But –'

'I mean it, now. Two weeks at least. Not a foot to the floor and I not giving you leave, or I'll not be responsible for what happens.'

Hugh gave in. Put that way, what option had he? MacDunleavy was not a man to exaggerate. Besides, now that danger no longer lurked round every corner, his reserves of strength had deserted him. He was exhausted. To be able to lie here in comfort, surrounded by friendly faces, lapping up the sounds and smells of liberty. It was an overwhelmingly enticing prospect.

He stretched himself with a luxurious sigh and asked MacDunleavy to send Eoghan O'Gallagher to him. To his surprise, however, it was not Eoghan who stuck his head round the door a short while late. 'Donal!' exclaimed Hugh, sitting bolt upright as his visitor entered the room. 'Donal Gorm MacSweeney! My God, is it really yourself!'

'It is,' grinned his friend. 'Ridden like the wild hunt all the way from Rathmullen to make sure you were safe home again. Sure, wasn't I starting to despair of you.'

'And you not alone in that,' said Hugh feelingly. 'Now, sit down till you tell me everything that is after happening in Tír Chonaill.'

Donal perched himself on the end of the bed. 'Everything, is it? And where will I ever start? How much is Hugh mac Ferdoragh after telling you?'

'Enough. I know my father is ill, that the country is split into factions, that the Englishman, Willis, and his men still occupy Donegal Friary. In God's name, Donal,' he drove a fist into his palm, 'why is no one after chasing them out?'

'Because Lucas Dillon had the truth of it,' said Donal grimly. 'We are our own worst enemies. Your father, God save him, is innocent as a child, and little better than a prisoner in what is left of Donegal Castle. Your mother is fled to the protection of The MacSweeney Doe, and the clan leaders, instead of supporting her, fight over the chieftaincy like dogs over a dead rabbit.'

'I will put a stop to it,' vowed Hugh. 'I swear it. As soon as I am well enough.'

There was a long pause. Donal fiddled with the cuff of his shirt and didn't look at him. 'That may not be soon enough,' he said at last, softly.

'What do you mean?'

'The Council in Dublin is already making mischief – each man of it desperate, no doubt, to avoid suspicion over your escape. They are urging Fitzwilliam to send an English sheriff into Tír Chonaill and he to support Hugh mac Hugh Dubh for the chieftaincy. We have to act now,

Hugh, drive Willis out. We have to show our strength – your strength.'

'But . . .' Hugh lifted his hands helplessly. 'I can't yet, Donal – I daren't. My feet – if I lose them I lose everything, and MacDunleavy says . . .'

'I know – I am after speaking with him. But –'

'And even Hugh mac Ferdoragh said I must not make a move till I was well. Surely, were things so bad . . .'

'Hugh mac Ferdoragh is not in Tír Chonaill. He does not see the things I see – hear what I hear.' Donal raked his hands through his hair. 'Ah, Hugh. Am I the reckless one? Am I Eoghan, to be urging you to rashness? The risk is terrible – I know it – but you have no choice. You are running out of time.'

Hugh bit his lip. 'But suppose . . . I mean, even if . . . what use would I be and I crippled like this?'

'You would be there – the returned hero, a champion for the clans to follow. You can still ride a horse.'

'Who will back me – apart from you and Eoghan?'

'O'Boyle would – Willis is after taking his castle too – and The MacSweeney Banagh.'

'Donchadh MacSweeney? But he supported Hugh mac Calvagh against my father. And my mother had mac Calvagh killed. The man must hate my guts.'

'Not as much as he hates Willis's. You are not after burning his homes and pillaging his cattle – and you don't have his hostages.'

'Hostages? Willis has hostages?'

'From every chieftain south of Bearnas Mór. How

else would he be getting away with what he does?'

Hugh closed his eyes. He thought of his injured feet – of what might happen if he ignored the physician's warning – and weighed that against what Donal had told him. Then he thought of his father. He thought of a bog on Inishowen and the hostages in Donegal Friary. He knew there was no choice.

'Fetch Eoghan to me,' he said grimly, 'and send out the call to the clans. We will ride before the week is out.'

Donchadh MacSweeney Banagh, encamped before the walls of Donegal Friary, came out of his tent to greet his newly arrived allies.

'A hundred thousand welcomes, Hugh Roe O'Donnell,' he said with a smile that didn't quite reach his eyes. 'It's glad we are to have you here – and you after travelling a rocky road to join us.'

Hugh steadied his horse and returned the man's stare. He wished that he could not feel his exhaustion stamped across his face for all to see. MacSweeney is testing me, he thought. Any sign of weakness and I am lost. Thank God I am on horseback, and he not knowing the truth of things.

'I am not here to join you, MacSweeney,' he said loudly. 'I am here to lead you.'

'Are you now.' The man's lip twitched sardonically. 'And you with all the experience of your nineteen years – and four of them spent in an English prison.'

'And my father's blessing on me, and half the country at my heels.' Well, it was close enough to the truth. His army *did* outnumber Donchadh's. And he had another advantage – or two to be precise – he had his champions. With Eoghan on his left hand and Donal – calm, dependable Donal – on his right, he could have stood unflinching before the gates of hell. 'The Unholy Trinity,' Eoghan had gleefully proclaimed them the day they rode out of Ballyshannon – and he had the truth of it. They had been through so much together, knew each other so well, they were like three sides of the same triangle.

He could feel their support, even without turning to look at them, and suddenly, as if reading his mind, Donal spoke. 'Is it for us to be arguing among ourselves?' he urged The MacSweeney, gently. 'And Willis's dogs watching us from yon walls? Hugh Roe has the truth of it – he has the larger force – but there'll be honour enough for all, I'm thinking, before this fight is over.'

MacSweeney didn't answer. His gaze flickered slowly over Hugh's assembled army and then shifted to take in his own camp. Hugh pressed home his advantage. 'How many of your people,' he asked, pointing towards the friary, 'lie hostage behind those walls? What counsel would they give and you asking them?'

For a long time the chieftain hesitated, but at last he shrugged his shoulders. 'You have the truth of it,' he conceded. 'Hugh mac Calvagh was my lord, and I'll not forget how he was murdered. But for now . . . sure, I can't fight two battles at the one time.'

He held out his hand and Hugh accepted it. A cheer went up from both armies, but Hugh was under no illusions. MacSweeney disliked him, the agreement would not be a lasting one – but at least it was a start. His first test of strength, his first victory.

That evening they held a council of war in Hugh's tent.

'I say we attack them,' declared Eoghan. 'We have the numbers. We could rush the gates.'

'A good move,' agreed MacSweeney. 'Or we could burn them out. Aren't they after strutting long enough like cocks on a dunghill?'

'And they after killing Brother Tadhg O'Boyle,' added Eoghan. 'Let you not forget that. Like a dog they cut him down and he in his own cloister. Let them pay for it. Let *them* feel the taste of cold steel in their bellies.'

He looked at Hugh and Donal, as if seeking support. Donal said nothing. Hugh felt his pulse quicken. Yes, he thought. Yes! Attack! Strike at the hated English, wipe out the humiliation of captivity – and let every blow be a knife in the gut of the English queen. But then he remembered something – the truth he had first understood that terrible day in Fizwilliam's torture chamber. This was not about him. It was not about honour or personal revenge. It was about survival. If he slaughtered Willis and his company, he would bring the English howling down on Tír Chonaill like the hounds of the Morrigu, and Tír Chonaill, faction-ridden and leaderless, would crumble like a burnt-out log.

He needed time – time to formalise his authority, to put his foot on the inauguration stone on Carraig na Dúin. Only then could he begin to forge unity among the warring clans. Yet, somehow, he had to confront Willis, and he had to win.

'This place is a house of God,' he said slowly. 'And a house of hostages. I will not spill Irish blood on consecrated ground.'

'Then what will you do?' jeered Donchadh MacSweeney.

'I will wait. We have them sealed inside those walls like rats in a barrel – we will starve them out.'

'Ha, the coward's way!'

'What!' Hugh sprang to his feet but immediately collapsed again. Before anyone else could move, Donal had risen in his place, and his sword-tip hovered at MacSweeney's throat. 'You will take back those words,' he told his kinsman in a voice as brittle as an ice shard, 'or I will force them down your throat, one by one on the point of this blade.'

MacSweeney's eyes bulged like a toad's. His face went from red to purple as he choked on his rage, but gradually he regained his self-control. 'My sorrow,' he said, unconvincingly. 'I am a proud man and quick to anger, it is not my way to be playing a waiting game.'

'Nor mine,' said Hugh, 'but bravery without brains is a dangerous virtue. This is not some cattle raid we are engaged on.' He looked at Donal. 'Put your sword up, Donal. The MacSweeney is sorry for the words he used. Is that not right, Donchadh?'

'It is,' conceded MacSweeney, though, once again, the message did not quite reach his eyes.

Donal sheathed his weapon and the conference continued, but the tension was still there. How long could this alliance hold? wondered Hugh. Would it be long enough to starve Willis into submission? Gambling had never been his favourite pastime and he had certainly never played for stakes this high.

The days dragged by. Boredom set in and everyone became tense and twitchy. MacSweeney said nothing but his thoughts were stamped across his face and written into every gesture of his body. The men grumbled among themselves and even Eoghan chafed at the inaction and kept pressing Hugh to change his mind. Only Donal remained his calm, unruffled self. How long dare I let this continue? wondered Hugh as each night followed another uneventful day. How far can I stretch them before I am forced to act?

Then seven days later, just when it seemed tensions must reach breaking point, the end came – quietly and undramatically. A man emerged from the friary carrying a flag of truce, and asked leave for his master to come seeking terms.

'Terms, is it?' roared The MacSweeney. 'I'll give him terms. I'll carve them out of his filthy hide and stuff them into his gizzard till he chokes on them.'

Eoghan backed him. 'They are beaten,' he urged. 'Now is the time to press our advantage – wipe them out like a nest of rats.'

Hugh and Donal looked at each other and shook their heads. 'Do you want to end up fighting the whole English army?' asked Hugh. 'Besides, they have prisoners. Would you risk their lives to satisfy your blood-lust?'

'And what of the friary?' put in Donal. 'Are we to hand it back in ruins to its rightful owners?'

For many hours the argument continued, but in the end common sense won out. Willis was ordered to appear before them and Hugh spelt out to him their conditions. 'You will leave with nothing but what you came with,' he decreed. 'No chattels, no livestock, nothing taken from this country. And the hostages you are after seizing – if I find even one of them harmed in any way . . .'

'They are alive and well,' Willis assured him hurriedly. 'And . . . and if we agree to all this, you guarantee to let us pass safely into Connaught?'

'You have my word on it.'

The Englishman eyed him suspiciously. 'How do I know I can trust you?'

'Am I a Saxon? When I give my word I keep it.'

'I will consider your terms,' said Willis.

Hugh was confident he would not refuse them.

Sure enough, a couple of hours later a messenger emerged to announce acceptance. There were wild celebrations in the Irish camp and, next morning, Hugh watched in silence as Willis and his men rode out. *Dhia*, he thought, if it could always be so easy. But he didn't deceive himself. He had won a minor skirmish, not a war. He tried to stir up a sense of triumph but all that came to him was exhaustion – and he had still to return to Bally-shannon, and a challenge of a different kind.

'I warned you,' said MacDunleavy gloomily. 'Rest, I said, and you charging off to Donegal instead. I told you I'd not be held responsible.'

'You did,' acknowledged Hugh. 'No one is blaming you. But –' he bit his lip, 'how bad are they?'

The physician shook his head. 'I'll not lie to you. It does not look good. The feet themselves I can save – I think – but those toes . . .' He shook his head again and touched one of Hugh's great toes with a pin. 'Can you feel that?'

Hugh shook his head.

'Or there? Or there?'

Nothing.

'They are dead,' said the physician. 'My sorrow, Hugh Roe, but they are beyond curing. I shall have to remove them.'

His toes – only his great toes. Hugh felt a surge of relief. Why did the man sound so concerned? He could live without two toes if he had to. He shrugged. 'Ah well, if you must, you must. Cheer up man. They're no use to me as they are, and sure there's not a glimmer of feeling in them. At least I'll not have any pain.'

'You don't understand.' MacDunleavy's voice was grim. 'They are starting to putrefy – like meat gone bad. If

I leave *any* dead flesh, it will poison your whole body. To take them cleanly, I will need to cut back to the quick.'

Mother of God! Hugh's stomach cramped. He jerked back his legs instinctively.

'I'll be as swift as I can,' promised the physician, 'and you'll have whiskey to deaden the pain.'

'And Donal and I will be here with you,' promised Eoghan. 'One each side and you to hang onto us if it is bad.'

'Wait! Stop!' Hugh's head was reeling. It was all happening too fast – another horror closing in on him, taking over his life. 'I'm not after agreeing yet,' he stammered. 'It's my decision.'

'But you *must* agree.' Eoghan stared at him open-mouthed. 'You haven't any choice – you know it.' He turned to the physician. 'You tell him again.'

'He has the truth of it,' urged MacDunleavy. 'There really is no other way.'

'Stop!' Why couldn't they let him be? Everyone telling him what to do again – knowing what was best for him. It was easy for them – they weren't facing the knife.

'Will you hold your peace, the pair of you,' said Donal suddenly. 'Hugh Roe has the truth of it. Sure isn't he O'Donnell in all but name? Is it our place to be telling him what to do?'

The others stared at him. Ha, that's telling them, thought Hugh. But as the seconds passed, he realised it was no lifeline his friend had thrown him. Donal was right, the decision *was* in his hands – but with choice came responsibility. Power was a double-edged sword – it could cut your own throat and you not using it carefully. Terrible things had been done to him in Dublin, but he had been a prisoner then and powerless. This time he must choose for himself. He must consent to this or he must die, but nobody could force him.

He lifted his head and looked into Eoghan's anxious face. He looked at MacDunleavy and thought of the knife and all the pain. Finally he looked at Donal. He took a deep breath.

'Pass me the whiskey,' he said.

The pain was white-hot – a molten river and he drowning in it. Even the whiskey barely dulled the edges. They poured it down his throat every time he surfaced and he struggled in a crucible of agony and alcohol. Time blurred. He heard voices praying – why did they plead for his life when all he wanted was to die? He moaned and screamed and writhed like a maggot on a griddle, unable to make prayers for himself.

Even his ghosts had deserted him. The nightmares took their place – John Bermingham in the cabin of the *Matthew*, Carew and his men at Castlekevin; the Constable in his butcher's booth below Dublin Castle. Pain and terror encircled him like serpents, crushing him till he could no longer breathe. Till his body exploded, flashed like gunpowder into blackness.

The pain ebbed and returned – but this time like an ember, its white heat dulled now to a glowing red. He lay without moving, feeling life run back into his body. His head burned, his muscles screamed, his feet were like two horseshoes plucked from the forge, but he had survived. He could feel a mattress under him, a pillow beneath his head. He knew where he was again. He opened his eyes and in the corner of his vision he could see Donal sitting beside his bed. Donal leaned forward, anxiously.

'Hugh, can you hear me? Are you back with us again?'

'I am,' he croaked. 'The little bit that's left of me.' And he tried to smile, but a wave of pain washed over him.

Donal reached out a hand. 'Is it very bad?'

'Like putting your feet into the fire. My toes – did he really take them, Donal?

'He did.'

'Then why do they hurt so much?'

Donal lifted his shoulders helplessly. He held out the whiskey jar. 'Will you take another drop?'

Hugh shook his head. 'It doesn't help – only to give me a pain in my head to match the one in my feet. *Chreesta*, I'm tired. How long am I after lying here?'

'Five days. We feared for you, Hugh Roe, and that's the truth of it. But your fever is gone and MacDunleavy says the wounds are healing cleanly.' He squeezed Hugh's hand. 'It's over, Hugh. You're alive, you'll walk again, the worst is past. It's over.'

Over? How could it be over, and he half dead with pain and his feet irreparably maimed? He had been robbed and cheated and shamefully ill-used – and he wanted vengeance. He lay in his pain and rehearsed his grievances – every abuse, every injustice, every wanton act of callousness that had brought him to this moment and this place. From the dark corners of his mind, he began to gather in his ghosts: Hugh mac Calvagh, Donnell O'Donnell, gentle Tadhg O'Boyle, Art mac Shane and the three hundred dead of the *Trinidad Valencera* – they advanced in a company of pikes and guns, and for the first time he saw himself at the head of them, leading them on his mutilated feet. He looked down a long black path into the future. Once he stepped onto that path there would be no turning back. And he would be alone as he had never been before. More solitary than a prisoner in his cell was a chieftain among his own people.

Had he the strength for it? He gritted his teeth and turned his head painfully, to look at Donal. 'You are wrong, Donal,' he said softly. 'It is not over, it is only just beginning. The old red English Morrigu tore apart a wasps' nest when she came poking her fingers into Tír Chonaill.'

Donal said nothing. He turned Hugh's words over in his mind and realised how little they surprised him. My soul, he thought, didn't I always know it must come to this in the end? He closed his eyes, and for a moment he, too, tried to peer into the future, but it eluded him. It was too dark – too shadowed with uncertainty.

He looked back at the bed. Hugh had fallen asleep again. His face was pale, the cheekbones far too sharp, the eyes deep sunk in blue and violet shadows. But the furrows of pain had lifted from his forehead and his body was relaxed – except for one curious thing. His right hand, upflung across the pillow, was curled into a fist, as though it held a sword.

Donal sat for a moment watching him, then rose and, stretching his own cramped limbs, crossed to the window to look out at the new day. The morning was cold and fine. The world beyond the window sparkled with hoarfrost, its whiteness pink-tipped by the first rays of the sun. A small wind ruffled the tops of the pine trees and high above them, little more than a speck against the lightening sky, an eagle soared on barely moving wings.

POSTSCRIPT

RED HUGH RECOVERED from his ordeal, though it was nearly a year before his feet were properly healed. In April 1592 his father abdicated and he was inaugurated as 'The O'Donnell'. In August of the same year he made a formal submission to the Lord Deputy. This was a meaningless gesture, however – four years of imprisonment had left him with a bitter distrust of the English – and within twelve months he had allied himself with Hugh O'Neill and Hugh Maguire in a struggle against the Crown that became known as the 'Nine Years' War'.

At first the Irish allies enjoyed great success, but a lack of resources and power struggles between and within the various clans made a sustained campaign difficult. They were promised help from Spain, but when, in 1601, the Spanish eventually landed an army, it was at Kinsale – on the south coast – while Red Hugh was in the north fighting a rearguard action against his treacherous cousin, Niall Garbh O'Donnell.

After an epic march across frozen terrain, Red Hugh

joined The O'Neill outside Kinsale and a battle was fought on Christmas Eve against an English force under Mountjoy. It was a disaster. The Irish plans were betrayed to the English; O'Neill, who had not wanted to fight, lost his way in a fog and failed to make the rendezvous, and the Spanish, for reasons known only to themselves, refused to come out of Kinsale and fight. The day ended in a resounding defeat for the Irish.

Red Hugh was devastated. He crossed to Spain to try to raise more help, but after six months of frustration and heartbreak, he eventually fell ill and died at Simancas on 10 September 1602 – a month short of his thirtieth birthday. There were rumours afterwards that he had been poisoned by an agent of the English Government.

And did he ever marry Róis O'Neill, the girl to whom he was supposed to be betrothed? Historians are still arguing over this question. A couple of English reports suggest he did, but they are unreliable and no Irish source mentions any marriage ever, to anyone. Father Donagh Mooney, who was with him when he died, stated quite categorically that 'he was not married', and certainly there is no evidence of any offspring – legitimate or otherwise. By the time Red Hugh died, Róis was married to Donal Balach O'Cahan.

main characters

THE IRISH

Hugh Roe (Red Hugh) O'Donnell, son of 'The O'Donnell' of Tyrconnell.

Donal Gorm MacSweeney, son of 'The MacSweeney' of Fanad, friend of Hugh Roe.

Eoghan O'Gallagher, friend of Hugh Roe.

Hugh Dubh O'Donnell, Hugh Roe's father, chieftain of clan O'Donnell and paramount chieftain in Tyrconnell.

Finnoula MacDonnell (the Iníon Dubh), Hugh Roe's mother.

Hugh mac Ferdoragh O'Neill (2nd Earl of Tyrone), claimant to the O'Neill chieftaincy and effectively the most powerful man in Ulster. Married to Hugh Roe's half-sister Siobhán.

Róis O'Neill, daughter of Hugh mac Ferdoragh, by his first wife.

Henry mac Shane O'Neill, cousin (and enemy) of Hugh mac Ferdoragh. Imprisoned in Dublin Castle with Hugh Roe.

Art mac Shane O'Neill, Henry's half-brother and fellow hostage.

Fiach mac Hugh O'Byrne, Lord of Ballinacor in the Wicklow Mountains. Ally of Hugh mac Ferdoragh and bitter enemy of the Dublin government.

Róis O'Toole: Fiach's wife, sister of Felim O'Toole of
Castlekevin.

Hugh O'Toole: brother of Phelim and Róis, fellow hostage of
Hugh Roe.

Turlough Buí O'Hagan, trusted emissary of Hugh mac
Ferdoragh, Hugh's guide on his journey back to
Tyrconnell.

Hugh Maguire, 'The Maguire', Lord of Fermanagh, cousin
and friend of Hugh Roe.

THE ENGLISH

Sir John Perrot, Lord Deputy of Ireland, reputedly the
illegitimate son of Henry VIII and therefore half-brother to
Queen Elizabeth I.

Sir William Fitzwilliam, Perrot's successor as Lord Deputy.

John Bermingham, a merchant of Dublin.

Nicholas Barnes, skipper of the merchant vessel *Matthew*.

Stephen Seagar, Constable of Dublin Castle.

John Maplesdene, Seagar's successor.

Richard (Dick) Weston, friend of Hugh mac Ferdoragh.

Sir Lucas Dillon, Member of the Dublin Council, a friend of
Sir John Perrot.

Henry Hovenden, Anglo-Irish landholder.

Richard Hovenden, Henry's brother.

THE SPANISH

Alonzo de Luzon, colonel in the Spanish army, leader of the
survivors of the Armada ship *La Trinidad Valencer*.

the o'neill family tree

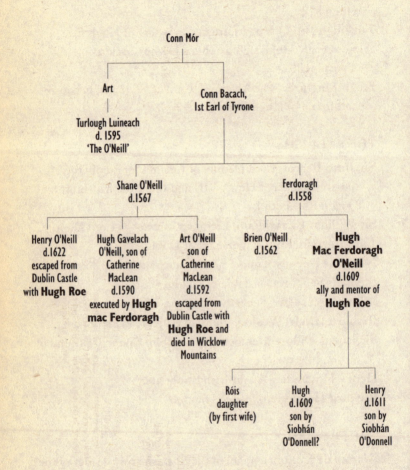

Conn Mór

Art

Conn Bacach,
1st Earl of Tyrone

Turlough Luineach
d. 1595
'The O'Neill'

Shane O'Neill
d.1567

Ferdoragh
d.1558

Henry O'Neill
d.1622
escaped from
Dublin Castle
with **Hugh Roe**

Hugh Gavelach
O'Neill, son of
Catherine
MacLean
d.1590
executed by **Hugh
mac Ferdoragh**

Art O'Neill
son of
Catherine
MacLean
d.1592
escaped from
Dublin Castle with
Hugh Roe and
died in Wicklow
Mountains

Brien O'Neill
d.1562

**Hugh
Mac Ferdoragh
O'Neill**
d.1609
ally and mentor of
Hugh Roe

Róis
daughter
(by first wife)

Hugh
d.1609
son by
Siobhán
O'Donnell?

Henry
d.1611
son by
Siobhán
O'Donnell

the o'donnell family tree

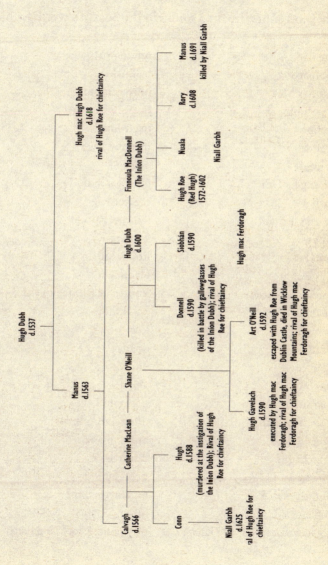

NOTE:

'ch' represents the final sound in the Scottish word 'loch'.

Amadán	omadawn
Ballinacor	ballinaker
Bearnas Mór	barnas moor
Brandubh	branduv
Brehon	breh-hun
Breifne	brefney
Calvagh	calva
Carraig na Dúin	corrig nuh dooin
Cashel	cashel
Cenél Chonaill	kennail kunnel
Chreesta	kreesta
Columcille	kolumkill
Connaught	konnucht
Conor mac Nessa	konner mack nes-sa
Cúchulainn	kookullin
Curragh	kurra
Dagda	dogda
Deirdre	daredra
Dhia	yee-a
Diarmuid	dearmid
Doire Leathan	durra lah-unn
Donal Gorm	dohnull gurm
Donchadh	dunn-a-ka
Drogheda	droh-hed-ah
Dubhdarach Roe	duvdarruch roe
Eoghan	oh-en
Eoghan mac Toole O'Gallagher	oh-en mack tool oh galaher

Fanad	fonodd
Felim	faylim
Ferdoragh	ferdorrah
Fiach	fee-yuk
Ficheall	fih-hull
Finn mac Cumhaill	finn mack cooill
Finnoula	finnoola
Geas	gas
Gráinne	grawn-yah
Hugh Dubh	hew duv
Hugh Gavelach	hew gavelugh
Iníon Dubh	Iníon duv
Lir	leer
Lough	loch
MacSweeney Doe	mack sweeney doe
Maeve	mave
Manus	manus
Melaghlen	melochlen
Miler Magrath	miler magrah
Mo chroí	muh cree
Mongavlin	mungavlin
Morrigu	morrigoo
Neill Garbh	nee-ul gorruv
O'Donnell Abú	oh donnell aboo
Róis	roe-ish
Slieve Roe	sleeve roe
Tadhg	tyg (long 'i')
Tadhg na Buille	tyge nuh bwilla
Tír Chonaill	teer conn-ill
Tír na nÓg	tcer nuh nogue
Tuatha dé Danann	toohah day donnunn
Turlough Luineach	turloch line-uch
Usnach	usnoch

More HISTORICAL BIOGRAPHY
from
THE O'BRIEN PRESS

STRONGBOW:
The Story of Richard and Aoife
Morgan Llywelyn

Winner Reading Association of Ireland Award
Winner Bisto Book of the Year Award (Historical Fiction)

The action-packed tale of the famous Norman knight who captured Dublin and married an Irish princess – Aoife, the King of Leinster's daughter.

Paperback £4.99/$7.95/€6.34

BRIAN BORU:
Emperor of the Irish
Morgan Llywelyn

The exciting, real-life story of hero and High King Brian Boru. Tenth-century Ireland is brought vividly to life as never before. Living history in story form, this book is accurate, exciting, entertaining and full of adventure.

Paperback £4.99/$7.95/€6.34

Historical Fiction from the O'Brien Press

KATIE'S WAR

Aubrey Flegg

Katie's father returns shellshocked from the Great War. Four years later another war is breaking out, this time the Civil War in Ireland. Katie's family is split by divided loyalties, and she feels there is no way she can help. Then she and the Welsh boy, Dafydd, find a hidden arms cache. Can they make a difference after all?

Paperback £4.99/$7.95/€6.34

THE GUNS OF EASTER

Gerard Whelan

Winner Bisto Book of the Year Eilís Dillon Award 1997
Winner Bisto Book of the Year Merit Award 1997

It is 1916: from the poverty of the Dublin slums twelve-year-old Jimmy Conway sees the war in Europe as glorious, and loves the British Army for which his father is fighting. But when war comes to his own streets, Jimmy's loyalties are divided. Looking for food for his family Jimmy crosses the city, avoiding the shooting, weaving through army patrols, hoping to make it home before curfew.

Paperback £4.99/$7.95/€6.34

A WINTER OF SPIES
Gerard Whelan

Eleven-year-old Sarah wants to be part of the rebellion in Dublin in 1920. But she doesn't realise that members of her own family play an important part in Michael Collins's spy ring, and her actions endanger them all. Sequel to the award-winning *The Guns of Easter*.

Paperback £4.99/$7.95/€6.34

FARAWAY HOME
Marilyn Taylor

Two Jewish children, Karl and Rosa, escape from Nazi-occupied Austria on board a *Kindertransport*. Their new home is a refugee farm in Northern Ireland. Here, they must learn to cope with the absence of their loved ones. Will they ever see their family again? Based on the true story of Millisle refugee farm in Ards, County Down.

Paperback £4.99/$7.95/€6.34

THE SHAKESPEARE STEALER
Gary Blackwood

A young boy is sent to steal Shakespeare's new play, 'Hamlet', but becomes involved with Shakespeare and his group of players. Will he betray his new friends and take the manuscript to avoid the vengeance of his brutal master?

Paperback £4.99/€6.34

SURVIVORS
Elisabeth Navratil

Two small boys, Michel and Edmond Navratil, are among the crowds waiting to board the ill-fated *Titanic* on her maiden voyage. They are excited, but their father, Michel Navratil Snr, is anxious – he has snatched the two children from their mother and they are travelling under false names to begin a new life in America. When the ship sinks, father and children are separated. What will happen to two boys with no names? Will they ever be reunited with their mother? *The true story of the lives of the author's grandfather, father and uncle.*

Paperback £4.99/€6.34

Send for our full-colour catalogue

ORDER FORM

Please send me the books as marked. .

I enclose cheque/postal order for £ . . . . (+£1.00 P&P per title)

OR please charge my credit card ☐ Access/Mastercard ☐ Visa

Card Number _ _ _ _ _ _ _ _ _ _ _ _ _ _ _ _

Expiry Date _ _ / _ _

Name: . . . . Tel: . . . .

Address:. . . . .

. . . .

Please send orders to: THE O'BRIEN PRESS, 20 Victoria Road, Dublin 6.

Tel: +353 1 4923333; Fax: + 353 1 4922777; E-mail: books@obrien.ie

website: www.obrien.ie